CONTEXTS

Authors:

Ann Bowen Carmela Di Landro Sheila Morris Olly Phillipson Sophie Yangopoulos

Series editor: Vincent Bunce

Longman Group Limited
Longman House, Burnt Mill, Harlow, Essex
CM20 2JE, England and Associated Companies throughout the World

First published 1995

ISBN 0582 27552 0

Set in Zaps Elliptical 11/14pt

Printed in Great Britain by Scotprint Ltd. Musselburgh, Scotland

The Publishers' policy is to use paper manufactured from sustainable forests.

Design and production by The Wooden Ark Studio
Illustrations by Terry Banbrook, Phill Burrows, Glen Marsh, Tony Richardson, John Stainton and Nigel Tyson
Picture research by Louise Edgeworth
Cover design by Ship
Cover illustration by John Clementson

Acknowledgements

We are grateful to the following for permission to reproduce copyright material:

Pages 88,89 CAFOD for adapted extracts from their leaflet Working in Partnership (CAFOD is the official overseas development agency of the Catholic Church in England and Wales); page 21 Friends of the Earth for an adaptation of the 'Campaign to Save Tropical Rainforests' advertisement.

In addition to the above small extracts or data from the following have been used:

Pages 10, 11, 30, 31, 50, 51,70, 71,82 and 90 from Population Concern Data Sheet 1994; pages 16, 24 and 25 from Brazil: a mask called progress by Neil MacDonald, published by Oxfam 1991; page 21 from Society Pieces by David Lambert, published by Cambridge University Press 1993; page 29 from Newsletter 33, published by Survival International 1994; pages 72, 76, 77, 84 and 86 from Countryfile Kenya published by World Aware 1994; page 93 from How do you see homelessness ? published by Shelter.

aWe are grateful to the following for permission to reproduce photographs:

Aerofilms, page 9 below; Art Directors Photo Library, page 26 below; Barnabys Picture Library, page 93; Ann Bowen, pages 30, 32, 46; CAFOD, pages 83 right (Sean Sprague), 87 below (Sean Sprague), 88 right (Anna Campbell-Johnston), 89 (Angelo Simonazzi); J. Allan Cash, pages 20, 25, 45, 55, 64, 90 above; Trevor Clifford, page 87 above; Colorific!, pages 18 (Paulo Fridman), 24 left (Mirella Ricciardi), 33 (Lee Battaglia); Colorsport, page 58; Lupe Cunha, pages 21, 92 above right & below; Sue Cunningham, pages 14, 19, 22; Fiat Auto UK, page 31 left; Robert Harding Picture Library, pages 26 above (David Lomax), 31 right (Robert Frerck/Odyssey/Chicago), 35 (Adam Woolfitt), 49 below (Peter Scholey), 62 left (G. Hellier), 72 (V. Southwell), 76 left (James Strachan), 84 below left and below right (Philip Craven), 90 below (Philip Craven); The Hutchison Library, pages 40 below, 82 (Liba Taylor), 83 left, 88 left; David Keith Jones/Images of Africa Photobank, pages 76 centre right & right, 78, 80; Sheila Morris, page 84; Network/Jenny Matthews, page 28; Nissan Motor (GB) Ltd, page 67; Oxfam/Robert M. Davis, page 24 right; Panos Pictures, pages 71 right (Trygve Bolstad), 81 above (Peter Barker); Science Photo Library, pages 4 above (Tom Van Sant), 4 below, 5 above (Earth Satellite Corporation), 5 below (Restec, Japan); Sealand Aerial Photography, page 9 above; Sony, pages 66, 94 left; Frank Spooner Pictures/Gamma, pages 52, 53; Still Pictures, pages 11 left (Mark Edwards), 12 (Paul Harrison), 17 (Mark Edwards), 27 (John Maier); The Stock House, pages 51 right (Ken Straiton), 59 (Jean Kugler), 61 (James Montgomery), 69 (David Ball); Tony Stone Images, pages 6 (Dennis Stone), 11 right (Pascal Rondeau), 43 above (Rosemary Evans), 50, 51 left, 54 (Chris McCooey), 56 (Matthew Harris), 57 (Paul Chesley), 62 right (Pete Seaward), 70 & 71 left (Mitch Reardon), 76 centre left, 81 below (Dennis Stone); The Sunday Telegraph Ltd, London, 1994/c Drew Gardner, page 47; Survival International/Steve Cox, page 29; TRIP, pages 15 (Eye Ubiquitous), 74 (R.S.Daniell); Telegraph Colour Library, pages 44 (Chris Bonnington), 49 above; Topham Picturepoint, pages 40 above, 48, 92 above left (Associated Press); UNEP-Select/Valter Anselmi, page 39; Zefa, page 94 right.

We are unable to trace the copyright holders of the following and would be grateful of any information that would enable us to do so, pages 43 below, 68 (photo: Paul Mulcahy).

We are grateful to the following for permission to reproduce artwork:

Page 13 Yanomami Land: from The Amazon Rainforest and its people, Marion Morrison, Wayland Publishers, 1993; page 25 Malaria cartoon: We are unable to trace the copyright holder; page 27 Curitiba's transport system: from The Geographical Magazine, June 1992; page 46 Map of Venice: © The Sunday Telegraph Limited, London 1994; page 48 The Migration Game: from The Active World, Manger & Readman, Thomas Nelson & Sons Ltd; page 73 The Baobab Tree & Page 79 The Maasai Rangelands: from Key Geography for GCSE Book 2 by David Waugh, published by Stanley Thornes (Publishers) Ltd; page 78 above Land use on Mwaniki's farm: from East Africa physical, regional and human geography by E.W. Young et al, published by Edward Arnold; page 78 below The Farming Year: from Lands & Peoples of East Africa, Hickman & Dickens, Longman; page 83 Matatu cartoon: Terry, Hirst. Matatu mode of public transport in metropolitan Nairobi. Mazingira Institute (Kenya) 1982; page 93 Shelter cartoon: from Shelter worksheet - No Home and Alone, Illustrator: Liz Pichon.

Contents

Our World

Brazil

Italy

Japan

Kenya

Development

Our World

Look at the four satellite images on these two pages … Can you guess where they are? Each one shows a country. The clues with each photograph should help you to identify the country. You may need to refer to an atlas to help you solve some of the clues.

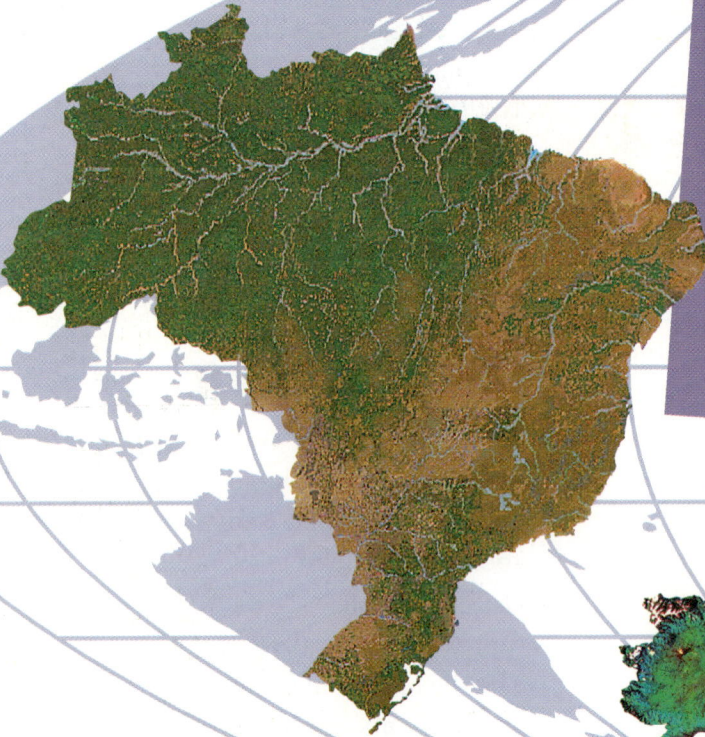

Clues

- 16.9 million hectares of this country's forest are being destroyed each year.
- In soccer, this country has won the World Cup many times.
- The Tropic of Capricorn and the Equator run through this country.

Clues

- *Ciao* means 'hello' and 'good-bye' in this country.
- It has its heel in the Mediterranean sea.
- Locate this country at latitude 42° North and longitude 13° East.

Clues

- You might find elephants if you went on a Safari here.
- This is large country in East Africa.
- The Tropic of Capricorn and the Equator run through this country.

Clues

- Your TV-set, Video or Walkman was probably made here.
- This country is the home of Sumo wrestling.
- Locate this country at latitude 36° North and 138° East.

Activity 1

a) Have you worked out the name of each country? Turn over to pages 6 and 7 and study the map (Source 3) to see if you were right. The four countries are highlighted.

b) In pairs, brainstorm and make a list of all that **you** know about each of the four countries.

c) What sorts of things do you think you might find out about each place?

d) What differences would you expect to find between these countries?

e) What similarities would you expect to find?

Finding your way

Continents countries and cities

Geographers are interested in many aspects of the world around them, but they are especially interested in places, and in what makes each place different. In this book you will be exploring four very different places – Brazil, Italy, Kenya and Japan. You will discover what makes each place unique and learn a little about what life is like for the people of those countries.

The **satellite images** on pages 4 and 5 are a new and exciting way of looking at the world. Another good way of finding out information about countries is to use maps and atlases.

Here we are going to concentrate on the three Cs … Continents, Countries and Cities. **Continents** are large land masses – Africa is a good example. **Countries** are usually smaller than continents and have their own government, currency, flag and sometimes language. Kenya is an example of a country. **Cities** are large towns within countries. They often contain the head offices of important businesses and services (such as banks) as well as cinemas and other kinds of entertainment. Capital cities are home to the government of the country. Nairobi is the capital city of Kenya. It might help to imagine the three Cs as a series of boxes, one fitting into another (Source 1).

Source 1

Continents, countries and cities

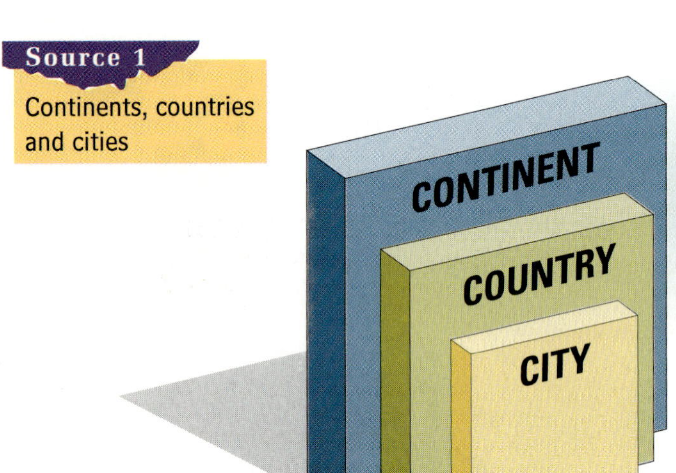

Activity 1

a) Draw three empty boxes, like the example in Source 1 and, using the world map, write in the names of a city, the country it is in and the continent where it is located.

b) Copy and complete the following sentences. Use this list to build up a glossary at the back of your book:

A city is …
A country is …
A continent is …

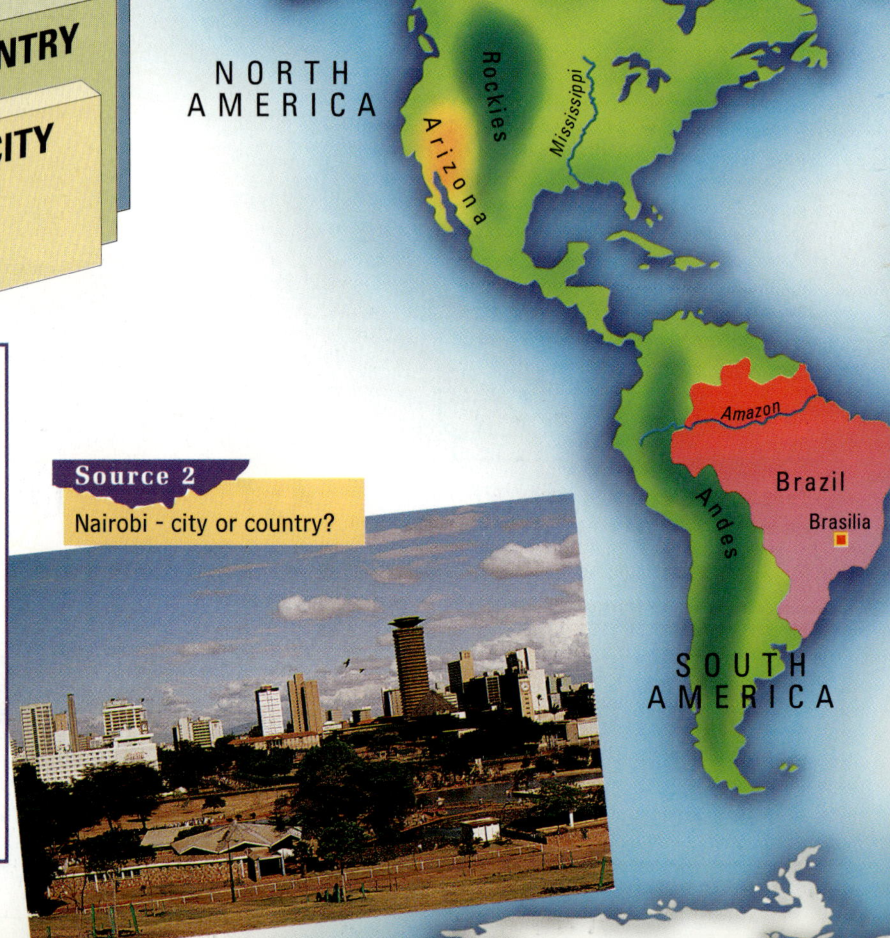

Source 2

Nairobi - city or country?

Highlighted on the map (Source 3) are the countries which feature in this book. The map also contains information about the world's physical geography. The main mountains, deserts, rivers and seas are labelled.

Activity 2

Study the map (Source 3) carefully:

a) What is the name of the country where you live? What continent is it in?

b) List the names of all the continents.

c) Copy and complete the table on the right for the five countries highlighted on the map. Use an atlas if it will help you.

d) Work with a partner to devise a quiz. Use the map to help you write five questions about places, for example:

- In which continent is the Nile?

Now close the book and test each other.

Capital city	Country	Continent
	Brazil	
	Italy	
		Asia
		Europe
Nairobi		

Source 3 Map of the World

A place you know?

Imagine you have been asked to find out about a place. Where do you start? In geography we are lucky because we can use a variety of information, including facts, figures, TV programmes, magazines, photographs, and of course, maps. You will have seen thc map in Source 1 many times before, but do you really know what it shows?

Is it a map of:

- The British Isles?
- The United Kingdom?
- Britain?

Source 1

Britain includes: England, Wales and Scotland.

The British Isles includes: England, Wales, Scotland, Northern Ireland, Eire and all the islands.

The United Kingdom includes: England, Wales, Scotland and Northern Ireland.

Activity 1

Study the map above and find the names of the following:

- the large port on the south coast;
- the river which has its source in Wales;
- the mountains north of Manchester and west of Leeds;
- a city on the east coast of Scotland;
- the sea that divides Britain and France.

Maps which only show major towns and cities are known as **political** maps. **Physical** maps highlight rivers, mountains and seas. What does Source 1 try to show ?

Still living on an island – think again?

Maps show us a great deal of information, but do they give us the whole picture? When we first look at a world map it is easy to think of the UK as an island. But take a closer look at the world map on pages 4 and 5. We are also part of a continent. Can you remember its name?

Now look at Source 2.

Source 2

Aerial view of Folkestone Channel Tunnel Terminal

Source 3

The European Union

Key
Member states
Countries wanting to join

Today there are two reasons why the UK is closer to Europe. One is the opening of the Channel Tunnel; the second is that the UK belongs to the European Union (EU). The UK joined the European Union in 1974. Today, the EU is a large and expanding trading community, as you can see in Source 3.

Activity 2

a) Name all the countries in the European Union.

b) Where are the headquarters of the European Union?

c) Look at Sources 2 and 4.

i) How would you describe each photograph?

ii) Compose a poem with the title 'No longer an island'. Use the poem to explain what it might mean for people in the UK to be 'closer' to Europe.

Source 4

Lunga, Argyll

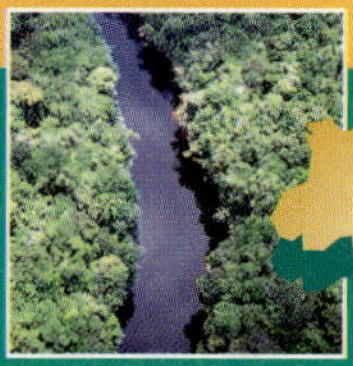

Brazil

What impressions does the word Brazil conjure up in your mind? You may think of coffee, of Rio's famous carnival, the national football team, or of Brazil's tropical rainforest, which contains the greatest variety of plant and animal life found anywhere on earth. What might escape you are the great contrasts in people and landscapes. Brazil is home to hundreds of different tribal groups. The landscape varies from remote rainforest areas (Source 3), to bustling cities like Rio de Janeiro (Source 4). Some of these contrasts will be examined in this unit.

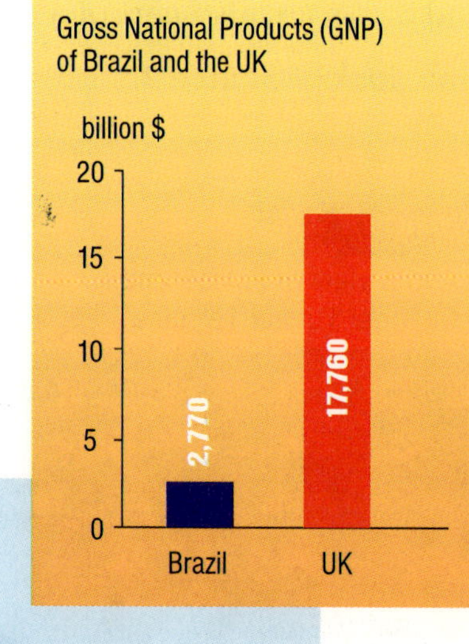

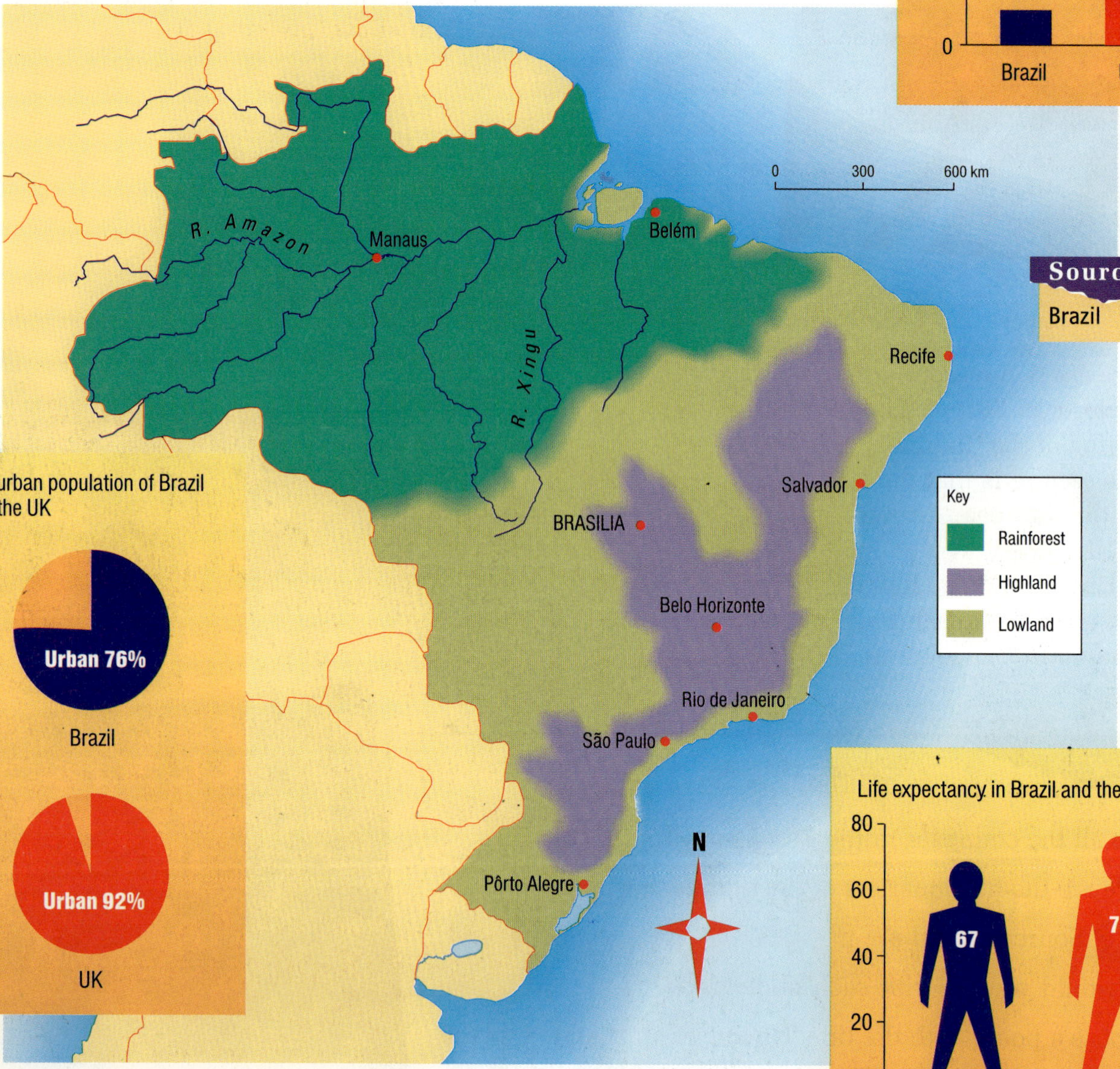

Gross National Products (GNP) of Brazil and the UK
billion $
20
15
10
5
0
2,770
17,760
Brazil
UK

R. Amazon
Manaus
Belém
R. Xingu
Recife
Salvador
BRASILIA
Belo Horizonte
Rio de Janeiro
São Paulo
Pôrto Alegre
0
300
600 km
N
Key
Rainforest
Highland
Lowland

Source 1
Brazil

The urban population of Brazil and the UK
Urban 76%
Brazil
Urban 92%
UK

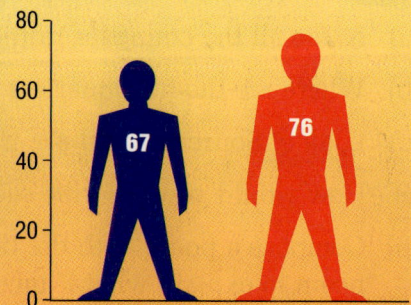

Life expectancy in Brazil and the UK (years)
80
60
40
20
0
67
76
Brazil
UK

Activity 1

Use the information from the map and an atlas (or encyclopaedia/CD Rom) to name these cities:

a) a city in the heart of the rainforest;
b) the new capital of Brazil;
c) the major port close to the mouth of the Amazon;
d) the old capital of Brazil (CLUE: there are three words in its name);
e) an industrial city in the south of Brazil.

Source 2

Brazil and the UK compared

	Brazil	UK
Population in millions	155.3	58.4
Area in km^2	8,456,505	241,595
Density of people per km^2	18.3	241
% population growth	1.7	0.2
Literacy %	82	99

Activity 2

Study the data in Sources 1 and 2.

a) Copy and complete these sentences, which compare Brazil and the UK.

Brazil has a population of ___________ which is three times as many people as the UK. The area of Brazil is 8,456,505 km^2 and so it is ___________ times larger than the UK. However, the UK is more crowded, with a population ___________ of 241 people per km^2.

b) Now use the rest of the information in the table and graphs to write sentences comparing the UK and Brazil in terms of:

- life expectancy;
- urban population;
- population growth;
- GNP (wealth);
- literacy.

Source 3

The river Xingu winding through the rainforest on its way to the Amazon. This region includes a National Park and is where many Indians live. The photo shows an undisturbed part of the forest, but a major road has been built through it elsewhere.

Source 4

Cidade Maravilhosa means, 'Marvellous City', in Portuguese and is the name given to Rio de Janeiro, Brazil's old capital city. Some 76 per cent of Brazil's population live in cities like Rio.

Population: growth, diversity and decline

Growth

Brazil is the fifth largest country in the world, with a population of almost 156 million people. Brazil's population is drawn from a number of different ethnic groups. Although the population is not growing as fast as it was, it is predicted to double to over 300 million in the next 40 years. The growth of Britain's population is much slower. It will take 281 years before there are twice as many people in Britain as there are now.

Source 1

The people of Brazil are very diverse

Activity 1

a) In which year is the population expected to double in:

- Britain?
- Brazil?

b) Study Source 2.

i) How long did it take for the population of Brazil to double from

1) 20 million to 40 million people?
2) 40 million to 80 million people?

ii) What is the predicted population of Brazil in the year 2010?

c) Study Source 3. Explain what has happened to:

(i) life expectancy;`
(ii) the infant mortality rate;
(iii) the birth rate;
(iv) the death rate.

d) Do you think the changes you have written about in c) will make Brazil's population grow faster or slower in the future? Explain your answer.

Source 2

Population growth in Brazil and the UK

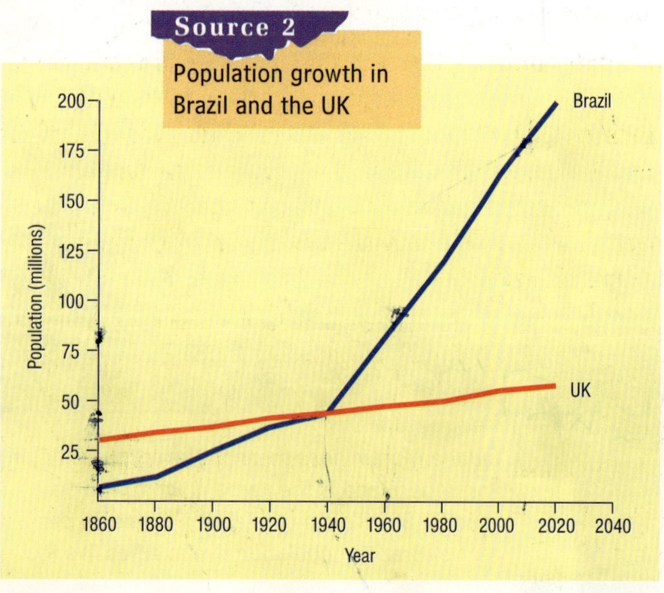

Source 3

Birth and death rates in Brazil

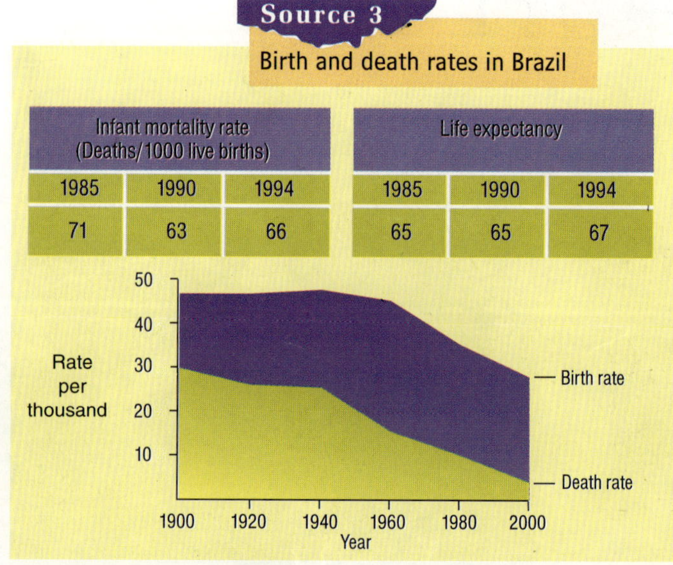

Infant mortality rate (Deaths/1000 live births)			Life expectancy		
1985	1990	1994	1985	1990	1994
71	63	66	65	65	67

Diversity

Many different groups of people live in Brazil. The original inhabitants are the Indians, who have lived in Brazil for over 3500 years. There are some 150 different Indian groups, speaking 100 different languages.

In the sixteenth century, the Portuguese came to Brazil and ruled the country until 1822. They brought West African people across the Atlantic Ocean to work as slaves on the sugar and coffee plantations. From the late 1800s other groups of **immigrants** came to Brazil. These included Germans, Italians and Japanese.

Source 4

The location of Indian groups in Brazil

Activity 2

Look at Source 4.

(a) Which Indian group do you find in the extreme north of Brazil near the River Branco?

(b) Describe the location of the Uru Eu Wau Wau Indians.

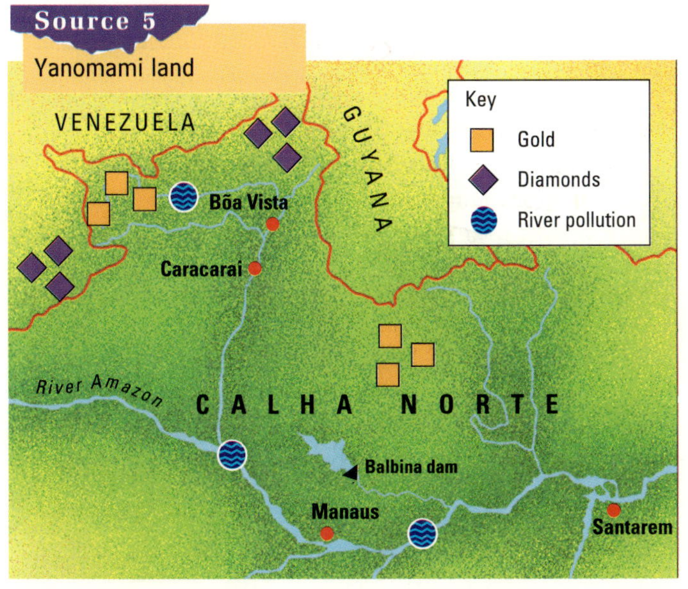

Source 5

Yanomami land

Decline

Many Indian groups in Brazil face extinction. Settlers looking for gold, diamonds, minerals and land for farming have brought diseases such as influenza and measles which kill the Indians. There were about five million Indians in 1500. Today there are only around 200,000.

In 1989, about 1,500 Yanomami Indians were killed by disease and violent disputes over land with miners. Although the Yanomami land was declared a protected area in 1992, the Yanomami only have the right to use the land. They are not allowed to own the land, and other activities still threaten their existence.

Activity 3

Study Source 5. What activities still go on in Yanomami lands? How might these activities harm the Indians?

Regional contrasts

Natural environments

Brazil has many contrasting natural environments (Source 1). The north-east is a dry region (Source 2) and suffers frequent droughts. The only vegetation which can grow here is thorn bushes or scrub land. This is known as *caatinga*. The north of Brazil lies across the Equator so it has a hot and humid climate all year round (Source 3). These are the conditions in which tropical rainforests grow best. In the centre and west of Brazil are vast tropical grasslands or *campo cerrado*. Sub-tropical pine forests are found below the Tropic of Capricorn to the south of Brazil. Further south again beyond the tropics are temperate grasslands called *pampas*.

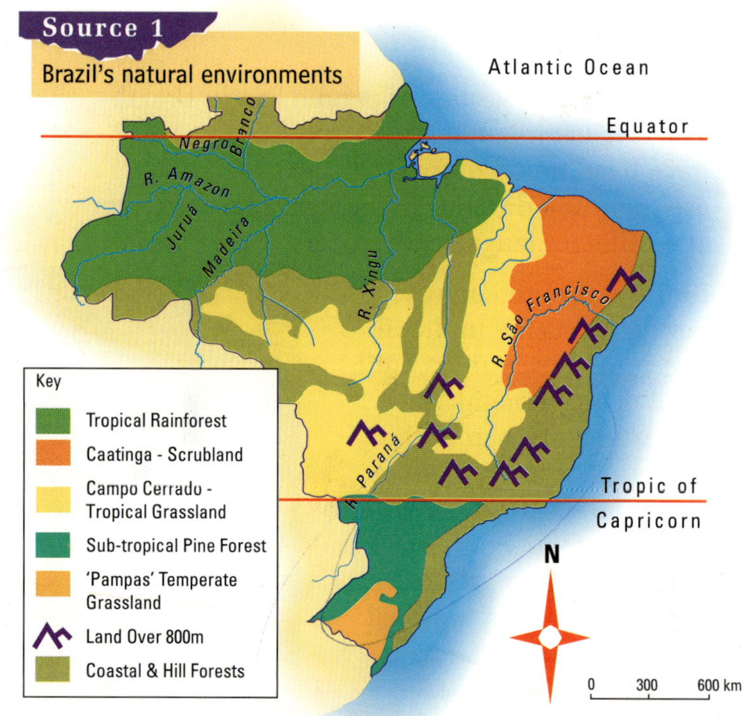

Source 1
Brazil's natural environments

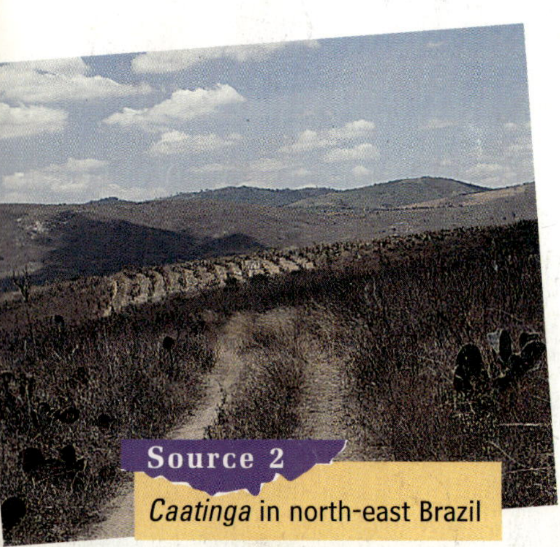

Source 2
Caatinga in north-east Brazil

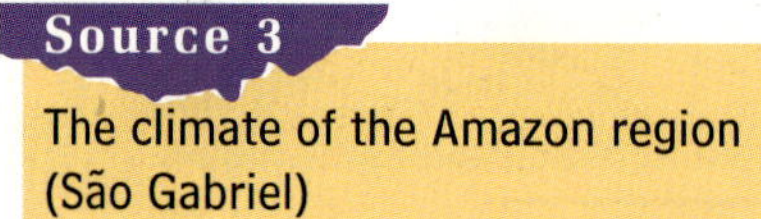

Source 3
The climate of the Amazon region (São Gabriel)

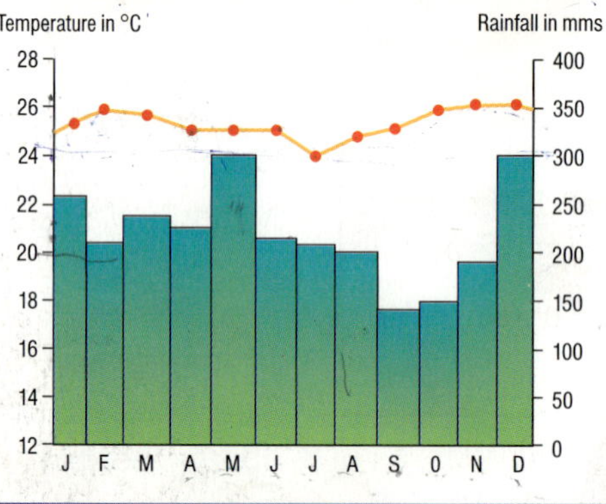

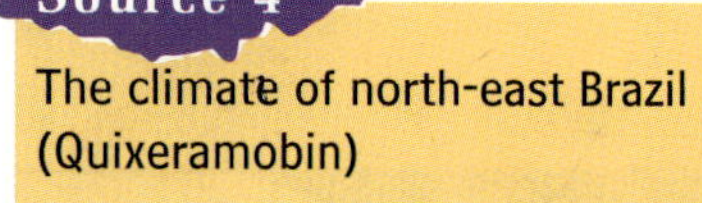

Source 4
The climate of north-east Brazil (Quixeramobin)

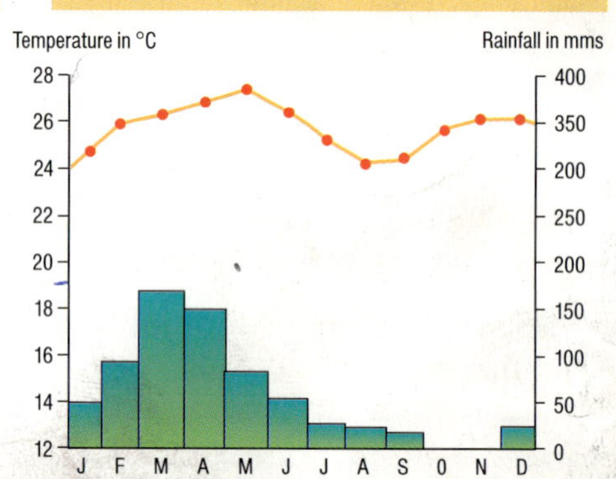

Activity 1

a) Study Sources 3 and 4. Describe two climate differences between north-east and the Amazon region.

b) Using the information in Source 5, draw a graph to show how the climate changes during the year in Rio de Janeiro. Use the same style of graph as in Sources 3 and 4.

c) Which months are the warmest in Rio de Janeiro? Why do you think they are different to the warmest months in Britain?

d) Look at Source 4 and at your graph of climate in Rio de Janeiro (south-east Brazil). Describe the main differences between the climate in the north-east of Brazil and the south-east.

Source 5
Climate data for Rio de Janeiro

	J	F	M	A	M	J	J	A	S	O	N	D
Temperature (°C)	26	27	26	23	21	21	20	21	21	23	24	25
Rainfall (mm)	124	124	125	105	75	50	35	40	65	75	110	135

Human environments

Source 6

Economic activities in Brazil

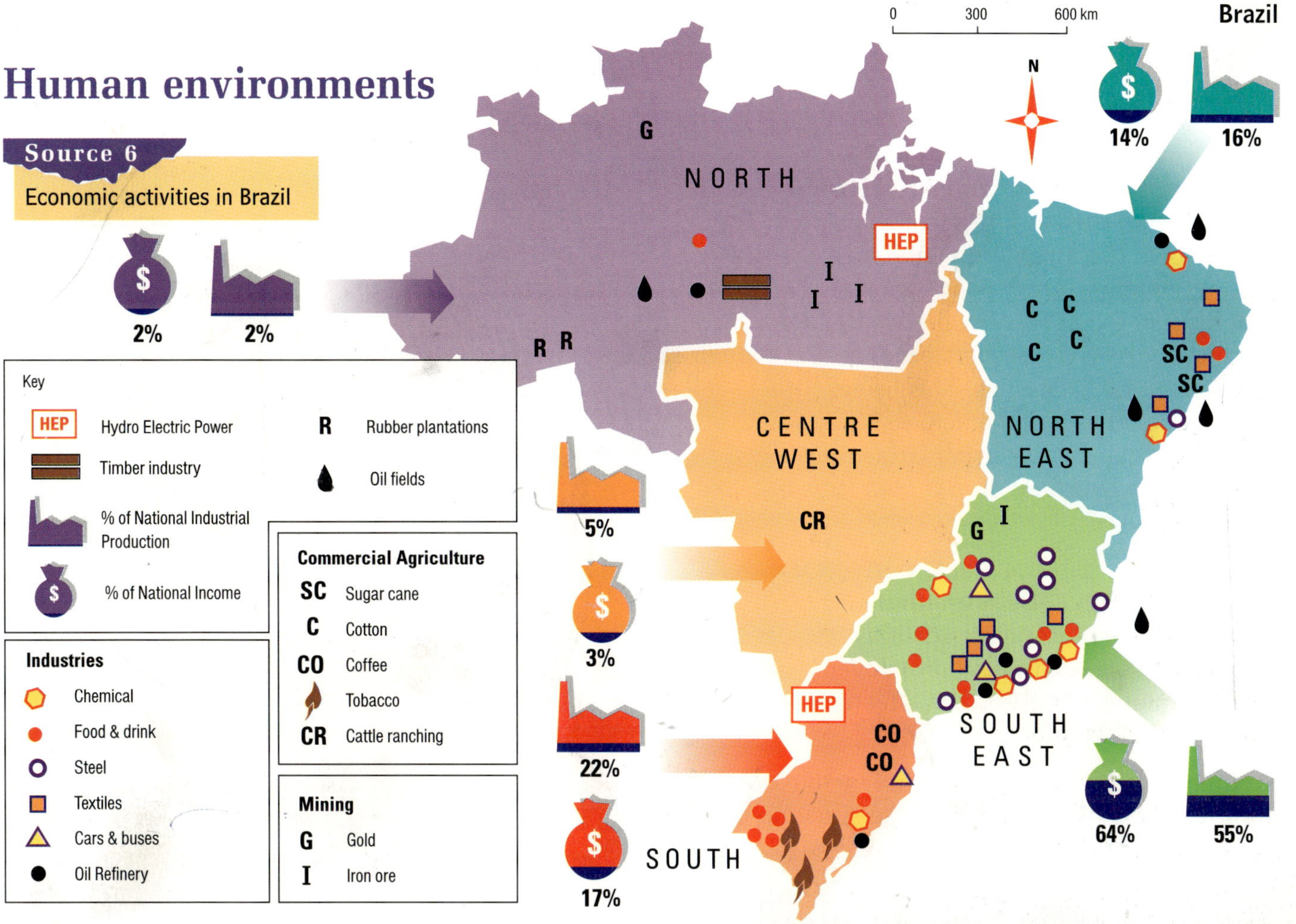

Brazil

0 300 600 km

N

NORTH: 2% (% of National Income), 2% (% of National Industrial Production)

NORTH EAST: 14% (% of National Income), 16% (% of National Industrial Production)

CENTRE WEST: 3% (% of National Income), 5% (% of National Industrial Production)

SOUTH EAST: 64% (% of National Income), 55% (% of National Industrial Production)

SOUTH: 17% (% of National Income), 22% (% of National Industrial Production)

G R R HEP I I I C C C C SC SC CR G I HEP CO CO

Key

HEP Hydro Electric Power

Timber industry

% of National Industrial Production

% of National Income

R Rubber plantations

Oil fields

Industries

Chemical

Food & drink

Steel

Textiles

Cars & buses

Oil Refinery

Commercial Agriculture

SC Sugar cane

C Cotton

CO Coffee

Tobacco

CR Cattle ranching

Mining

G Gold

I Iron ore

Source 7

An industrial complex in Minas Gerais

Although most people live in the north-east and south-east of Brazil, industry and farming takes place in most parts of the country. Some of the fastest growing cities are now in the Amazon region where mining, hydro-electric power and logging provide jobs for people and money for Brazil to develop. These activities often result in the natural environment being changed:

- In the south of Brazil, the natural grasslands have been replaced by tobacco plantations.
- Soft wood timber is cut from the sub-tropical pine forests.
- The largest hydro-electric power plant in the world (Itaipu) on the Paraná river, has flooded thousands of square kilometres of land.

People have changed natural landscapes into human landscapes.

Activity 2

a) Study Source 6. What are the main economic activities in:

i) north-east Brazil;

ii) south-east Brazil?

b) Which region makes the most money for Brazil?

Rural lives

In Brazil just 4 per cent of the population own 67 per cent of the land. In the north-east, rich farmers own the most fertile land near the coast. On the remaining land, poor farmers grow small quantities of food. This is called **subsistence farming** because the farmers produce just enough food to feed their families. This leaves little to sell to pay for clothes and medicines. Many small farmers rent land from a rich farmer and pay a third or even half their crop in rent (this is called **sharecropping**).

Drought is another problem for farmers in the north-east of Brazil. **Deforestation** may be to blame for more frequent droughts affecting farmers in this region. In 1992 the drought area covered one million square kilometres and affected nine million people.

Antonio Alves, a small farmer and member of the Rural Workers Union describes the situation of poor farmers:

'The rains have been coming late and the amount of rainfall is less. There used to be a lot of trees around here. Now they've been cut down. The only land we can get is on the tops of hills. All the good low land is planted to sugar cane.'

Source 1

Who owns the land in Brazil?

FARMLAND IN BRAZIL

Activity 1

Use Source 2 to write a description of how deforestation might cause droughts.

Source 2

Deforestation and drought

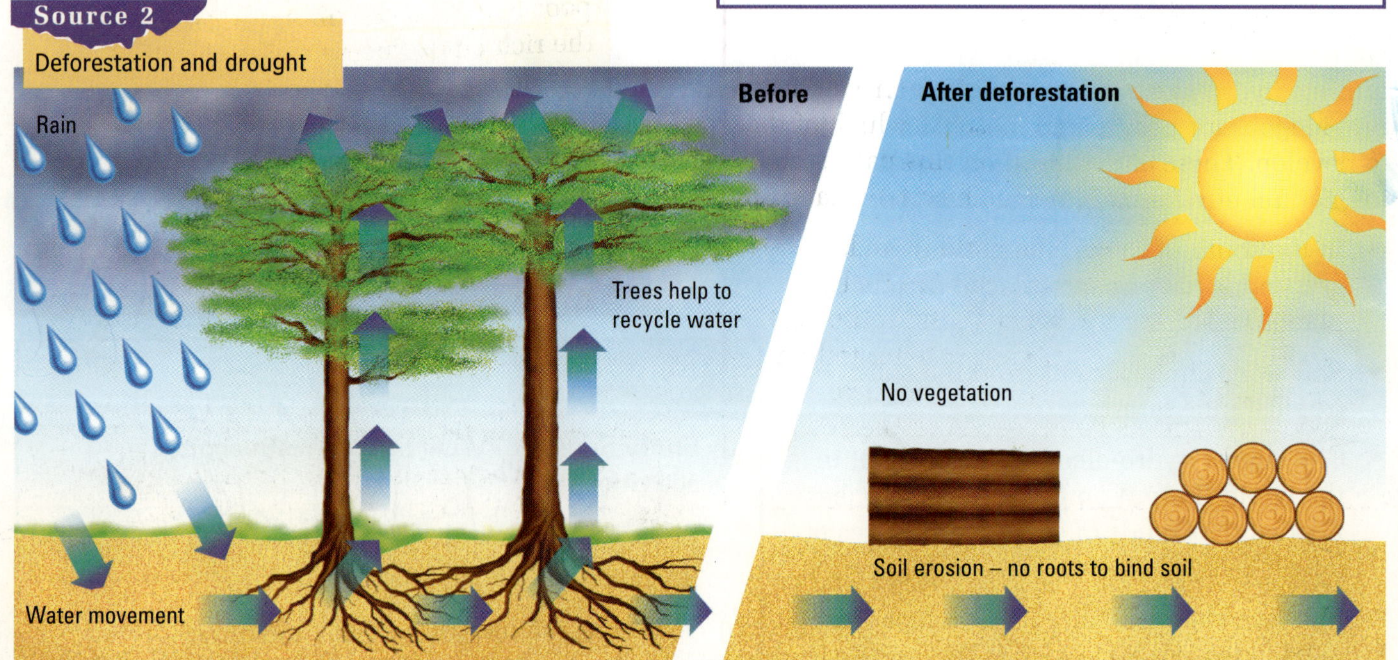

Source 3

Subsistence farmers in Brazil

Relief aid

The government of the north-east state of Pernambuco has promised £5 million to help farmers in times of drought. The money will help provide water (which will be transported to the region by lorries), and emergency food handouts of rice, beans, sugar and cooking oil.

Irrigation projects

A foreign bank will give the Brazilian government a loan of £18 million to **irrigate** farmland in the north-east with water from the São Francisco valley. Two thousand acres will be sold to farmers.

Land reform

Brazilian law says that abandoned land which is not farmed should be given to poor farmers who will use it. However, the rich landowners argue about this and do not want to give up their land, even though they don't use it. The Landless People's Movement of Paraiba is an organisation which helps poor farmers to get land. They will own this land and so will not have to pay rent.

Solutions

On the right are three possible solutions to the problems facing farmers in the north-east of Brazil.

Group Activity

a) Imagine you are a group of poor farmers in the north-east of Brazil. Discuss which of the three solutions discussed on this page would help you the most over the next ten years.

b) You have a friend who could not make enough money to support his family by farming. He went to a city in the south-east of Brazil to find work. Write a letter to him describing how the solutions you have chosen might make life easier in the north-east.

Deforestation: the removal of trees in an area.

Fertile: land which is rich in nutrients and good for growing crops.

Subsistence farming: farming which provides just enough food for the farmer and family, leaving little or no surplus.

Industry in Cubatão

Most of the industries in Brazil like steel, chemicals and car production are in the south-east of the country where there are:

- good road and rail networks for transporting goods;
- two large ports (Rio de Janeiro and Santos) for shipping goods to other countries;
- many large cities providing a workforce and a market for selling manufactured goods;
- coal, nuclear and hydro-electric power stations providing electricity for industry.

South-east Brazil has earned money from its industries, but they have also caused problems. Many industries are owned by foreign companies which take most of the profits they make out of Brazil. Workers are often paid low wages and there are few pollution controls.

Source 1

Cars being exported at the port of Rio

The Valley of Death

Cubatão is a town located between São Paulo and Santos. Until recently it was named 'the valley of death' and 'the most polluted place on earth'.

The situation in Cubatão shows how industrial development can lead to environmental disaster (see Source 2).

Activity 1

a) Study Sources 2 and 3.

i) Where is the pollution coming from?
ii) What are the dangers for people building houses on the valley sides?

b) From the information on this page write a poem about the valley of death. Before you start, try and complete the sentences below, to give you ideas for completing the poem.

Verse 1 *The industry came to Cubatão …*
(Why is it a good location?)

Verse 2 *People followed industry to Cubatão...*
(Why did they come and where did they live?)

Verse 3 *Smoke filled the air over Cubatão …*
(How did this affect the environment and people?)

Source 2

Cubatão – the valley of death

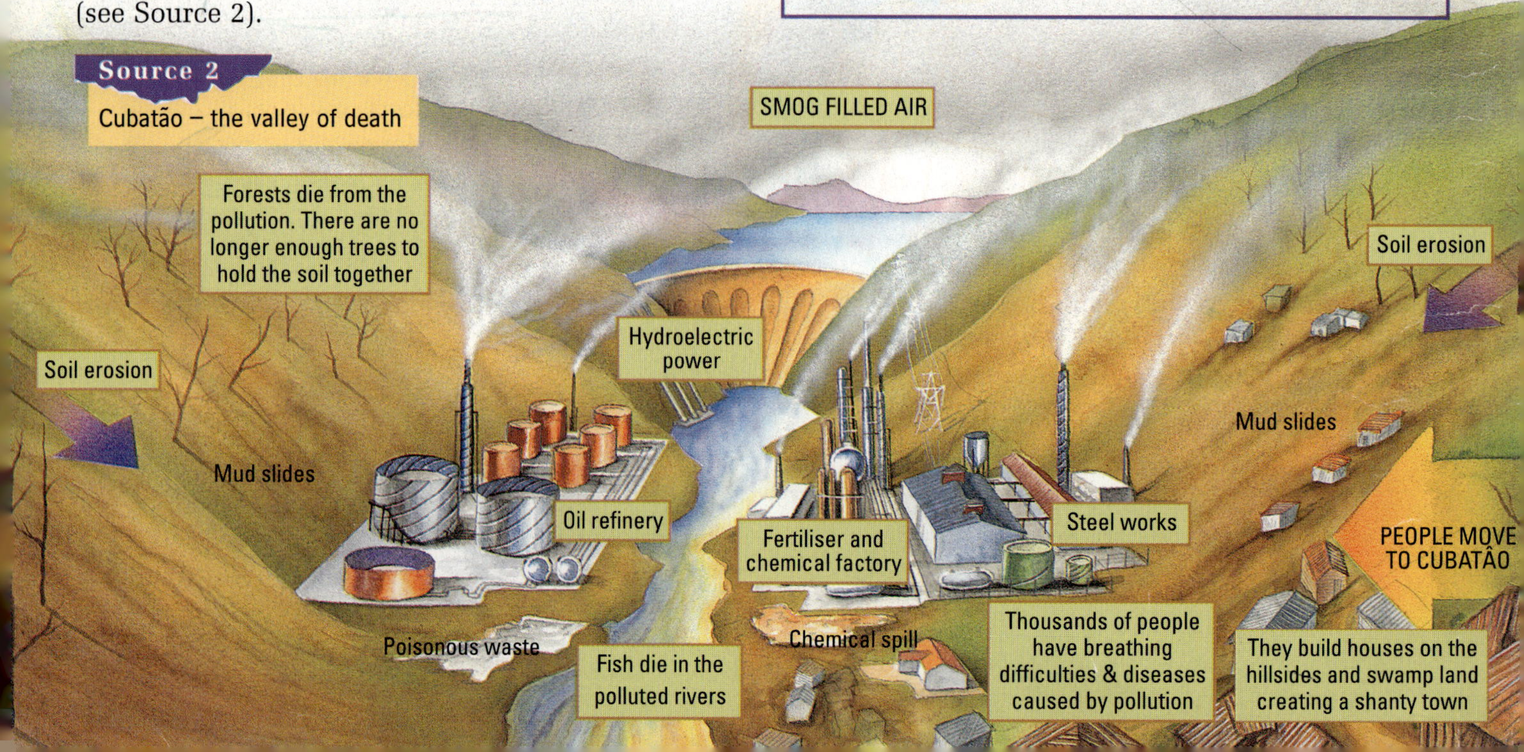

SMOG FILLED AIR

Forests die from the pollution. There are no longer enough trees to hold the soil together

Soil erosion

Hydroelectric power

Mud slides

Oil refinery

Fertiliser and chemical factory

Steel works

Soil erosion

Mud slides

PEOPLE MOVE TO CUBATÃO

Poisonous waste

Fish die in the polluted rivers

Chemical spill

Thousands of people have breathing difficulties & diseases caused by pollution

They build houses on the hillsides and swamp land creating a shanty town

The clean up

The local government decided to clean up the 'valley of death'. It cost US$220 million. Half of this money was raised from a World Bank loan. Industries reduced pollution by using special equipment. They cleaned up 78 per cent of all the sources of pollution and improved river water quality. They planted trees on the mountain slopes to prevent **soil erosion**. Despite this success, the government-owned steel works still pollutes the valley. It can't afford pollution control equipment because all its profit is being used to pay back some of Brazil's debts.

Source 3

Cubatão

Source 4

Brazil's debt and environment cycle

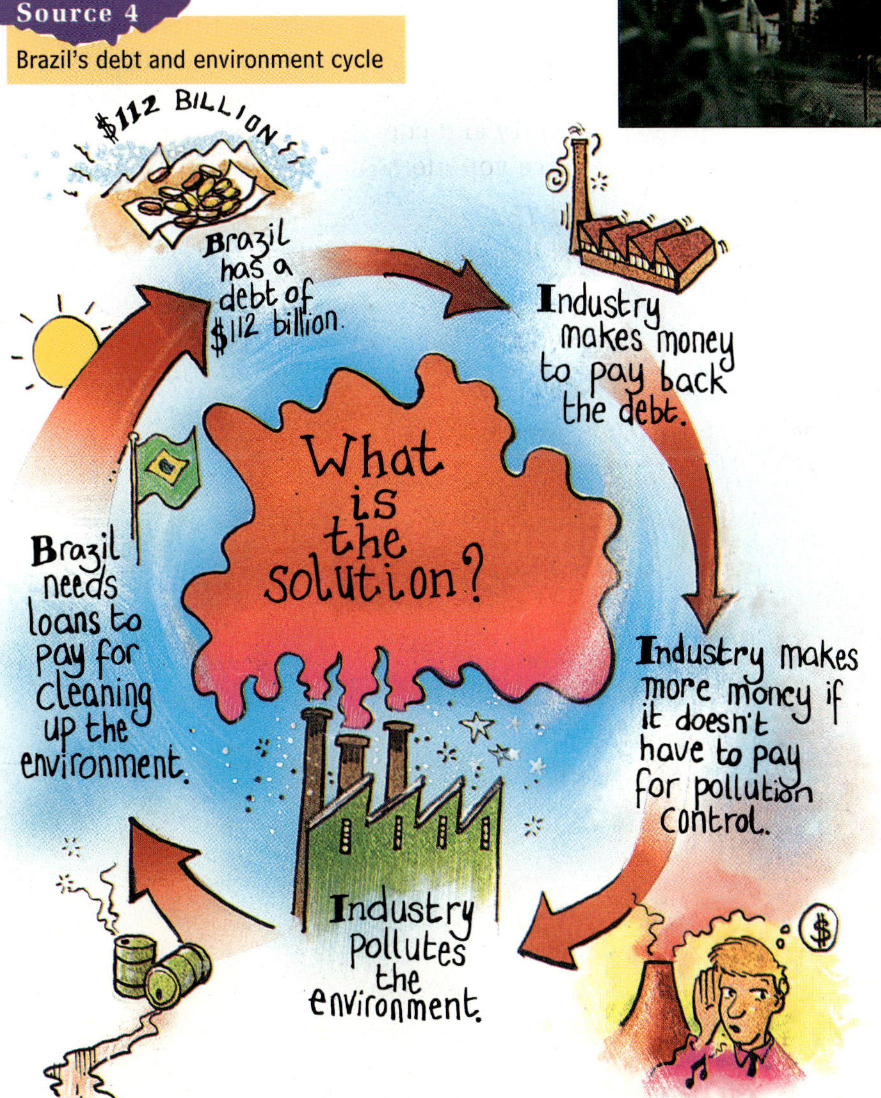
$112 BILLION
Brazil has a debt of $112 billion.
Industry makes money to pay back the debt.
Industry makes more money if it doesn't have to pay for pollution control.
Industry pollutes the environment.
Brazil needs loans to pay for cleaning up the environment.
What is the solution?

Activity 2

a) Why do you think it is so difficult to completely clean up Cubatão's environment?

b) Source 4 shows how Brazil finds it difficult to prevent environmental damage while it still has debts.

Imagine you are the Brazilian Environment Minister. Write a letter to an international bank persuading it to cancel Brazil's debt.

The timber trade: winners and losers

Source 1

Logging in the Amazon

Brazil needs money for development. It can earn money by selling goods to other countries. This is called **international trade**. The goods sold abroad are called exports and the money earned is called **foreign exchange**.

Mahogany

One of Brazil's exports is mahogany wood (Source 2). Britain buys 52 per cent of all Brazilian mahogany trees felled. Brazil depends on Britain for money from the sale of wood. Britain depends on Brazil for a raw material (mahogany logs) to make things such as stairs, kitchen cupboards and even toilet seats. This link between countries is sometimes called **interdependence**.

Activity 1

Write down the name of any manufactured product you use at home and the raw material it is made from. Does the raw material or manufactured product come from another country?

Source 2

The mahogany timber trade

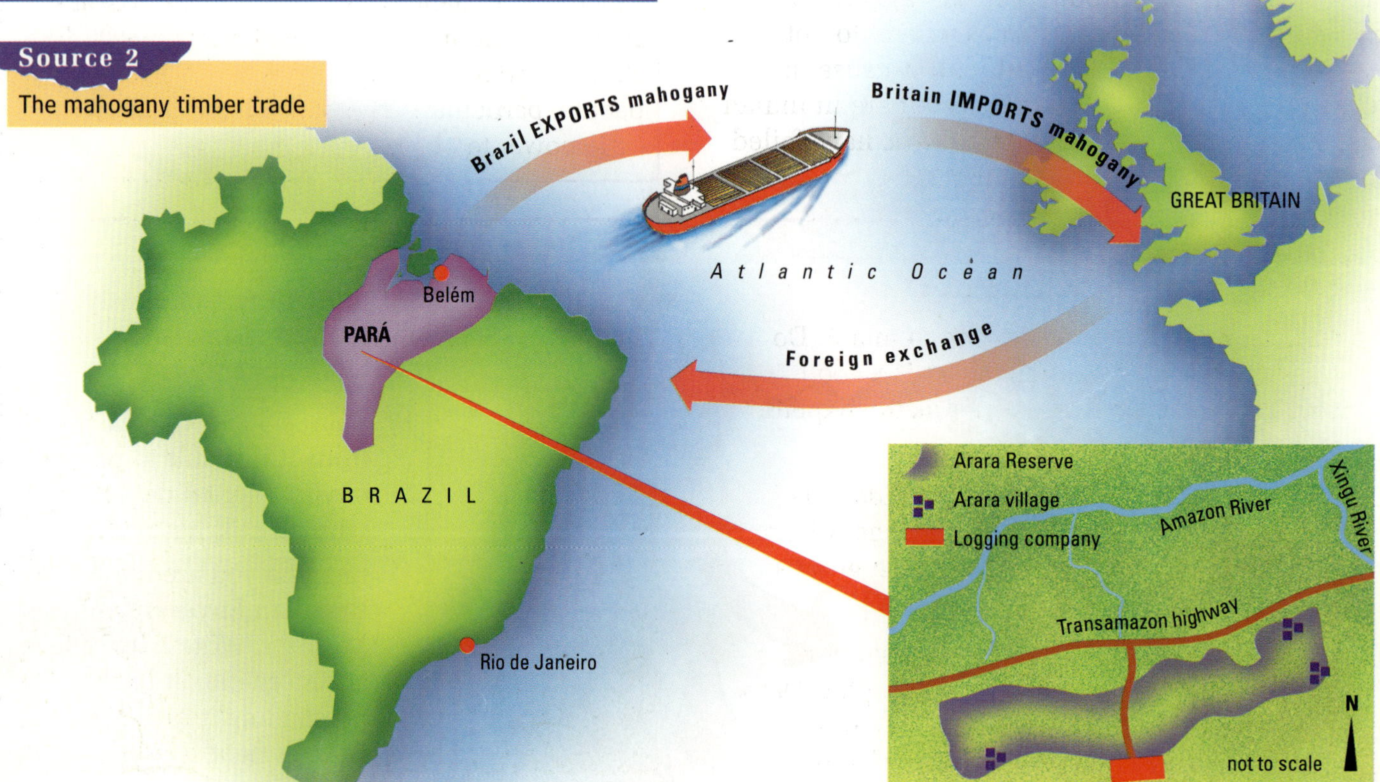

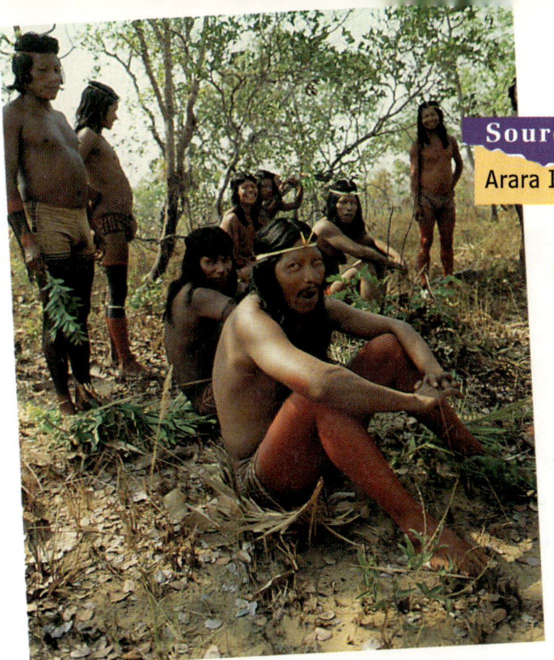

Source 3
Arara Indians

Source 4
An advertisement asking people not to buy hardwood products

EVERY YEAR 11 MILLION ACRES OF RAINFOREST ARE DESTROYED FOR THE SAKE OF CONVENIENCE

It's not just fashionable mahogany toilet seats that are to blame. Doors, floors, window frames and household furniture - every product made of tropical hardwood contributes to this destruction.

Hardwood products are available in every high street in every town.

In Britain we can greatly help by refusing to buy tropical hardwood products.

It took 100 million years to create the tropical rainforests but only 40 years to destroy half of them. If we don't act now there will be none left in another 40 years.

CAMPAIGN TO SAVE TROPICAL RAINFORESTS

FRIENDS OF THE EARTH

Mahogany trees grow in the Amazon, but most have now been cut down. Timber companies are now cutting down mahogany trees illegally from inside protected Indian lands such as the Arara Indian Reserve in Pará. The Arara people are forced to live on the edge of the reserve because loggers have moved in to the rest of it. In 1970 there were 400 Arara Indians. Today only 130 are left because the environment on which they depend is being destroyed.

DIY stores in Britain say that from 1995 they will not sell mahogany products which they have bought from logging companies which do not replant trees. This will be difficult because the only places with mahogany trees left are in Indian reserves, and attempts to replant trees have failed because pests damage the young trees.

Source 5
Sustainable development

Sustainable development is the ability of one generation to hand over to the next at least the same amount of resources as it started with. It should also be development which helps all people, particularly the poorest and those with little power to change their own lives.

Activity 2

Read the information in Sources 4 and 5. Do you think the trade in mahogany is a good example of sustainable development? Explain your answer.

a) In small groups discuss and decide which groups in the table on the left benefit from the trade in mahogany and which groups lose out.

b) Copy and complete the table to show your decisions on a large poster for display. Draw pictures around the chart to show the reasons why each group gains or loses.

The timber trade: winners and losers

	winners	losers
The Arara Indians		X
Brazilian logging companies		
The Brazilian Government		
British importers		
British DIY stores		
British consumers (people who buy mahogany products)		

Alternative trading: Brazil nut oil

Trade between countries can contribute to **sustainable development**. It can benefit small communities and take place without destroying the environment. The Kayapó Indians in the Amazonian region of Pará have been trading successfully with The Body Shop since 1991.

The Kayapó Indians wanted to sell rainforest products so that they could buy fishing lines, an outboard motor and medicines to cure diseases brought in by white people. After discussions, the Kayapó agreed to sell Brazil nut oil to The Body Shop, who use it to make hair conditioner.

Brazil nuts are collected between January and March. It is a community activity. The oil is extracted by a hand-operated press purchased by the Kayapó with a loan from The Body Shop. The price of Brazil nut oil was worked out and agreed jointly.

Source 1

Making Brazil nut oil

Source 2

Kayapó villages in Brazil

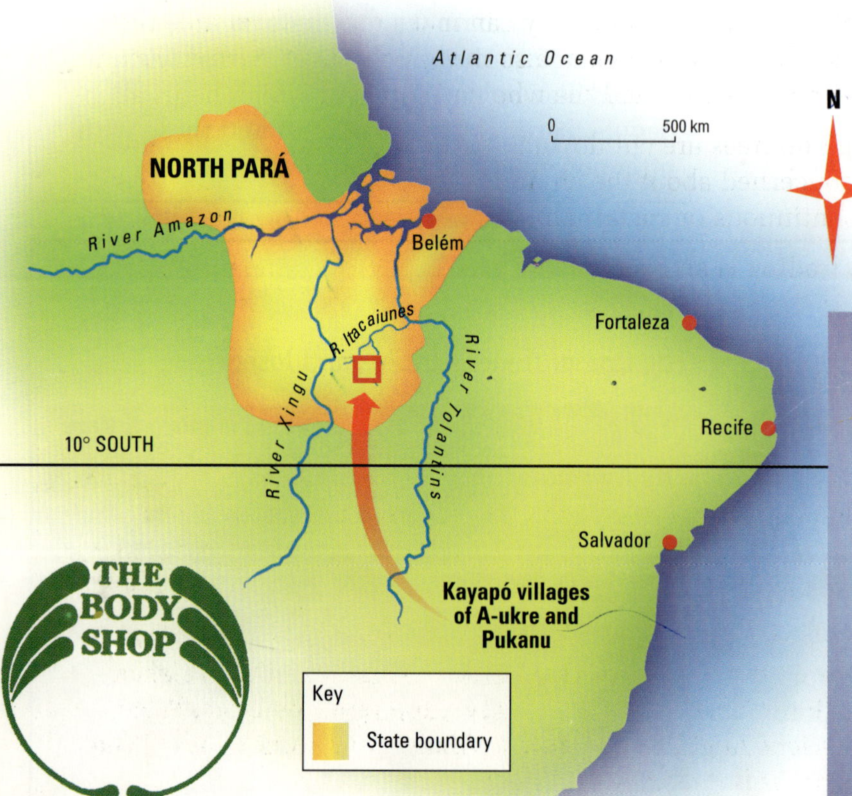

Activity 1

Describe the location of the Kayapó villages in Source 2. In your answer include where in Brazil they are, and which rivers they are near to.

Source 4

Growing Brazil nuts

The trees are over 40 metres tall. About five nuts grow inside an 'Ourico' a coconut type shell.

Source 5

Sustainable development should:

1 respect all environments and cultures;
2 use traditional skills and local knowledge;
3 give people control over their land and lives;
4 use appropriate technology – machines and equipment that are cheap, easy to use and do not harm the environment;
5 generate income for communities by giving them fair prices for the products they sell (trade).

Other rainforest products

If Brazil nut oil conditioner goes out of fashion in Britain and people do not buy it, the Body Shop may stop making it. The Kayapó would not be able to sell their oil and so would not make any money. To make sure they do not depend on only one product, the Kayapó are using their expert knowledge to find other forest products which they can trade, such as natural dyes and insect repellants. If one product does not sell well in Britain they can make money from the other products. The Kayapó women also make wristbands to trade, making money for themselves and the whole village.

Although no trees are cut down to make Brazil nut oil, the Body Shop is still concerned about the environment. It checks that the trees can give a continuous or **sustainable** supply of nuts well into the future.

Kayapó trading is an example of sustainable development.

Activity 2

a) Which rainforest activities or trading agreements described on these pages are examples of points 1 to 5 in Source 5? For example, the Body Shop respects the environment (point 1) by checking that the trees can give a continuous supply of nuts.

b) Other Kayapó villages are showing interest in trading. Write, then act out a conversation between Chief Paulinho Paiakan, another village chief and a Body Shop representative. What questions might the interested village chief want to ask? What replies will the chief get in return?

Amazon gold rush

In the last few years, over one million people looking for gold, or *garimpeiros*, have gone to the Amazon to find their fortune. However, most never become rich because they work for 'gold barons' who keep most of the profits.

Gold is found by clearing patches of rainforest. After the valuable metal is dug out of the ground, large ugly red-brown scars are left on the land. The soil is easily washed by rain into rivers, choking them up. This increases the risk of flooding. Gold is also found in the sediment at the bottom of rivers. Engines on floating platforms pump up the sediment containing gold from the river bed.

Source 1

Areas of high *garimpeiro* activity in Brazil

Source 3

Amazon gold mine

Source 2

Davi Yanomami

Davi Yanomami, an Indian leader, describes how gold mining causes environmental problems and how people are affected:

'At first the garimpeiros tried to make friends with the Yanomami. Then the Yanomami saw that they were being tricked. When the forest is gone, the only food available is the food the garimpeiros bring so they can make the Yanomami work for a plate of food. They make people drink and they get used to the alcohol and get sick.'

'They are destroying the rivers with mercury and oil from the machines. The fish that we eat and the water we drink make us sick.'

Source 4

Dredgers on the Madeira River

Extracting gold can harm the environment. Mercury is used to attract the gold from the river sediment. The mercury is then burned off and enters the atmosphere. It is rained back down, and helps to poison streams and rivers.

Source 5

The Rondonia State newspaper *Estado* notes the growing problem of malaria. The text reads:

Malaria: up until April, 92 thousand cases have been confirmed in the state.

Cartoon: Why so many legs if it can fly?

Rondonia is the Brazilian state with the greatest number of cases of malaria, with more than 200,000 cases confirmed by the government department dealing with public health campaigns.

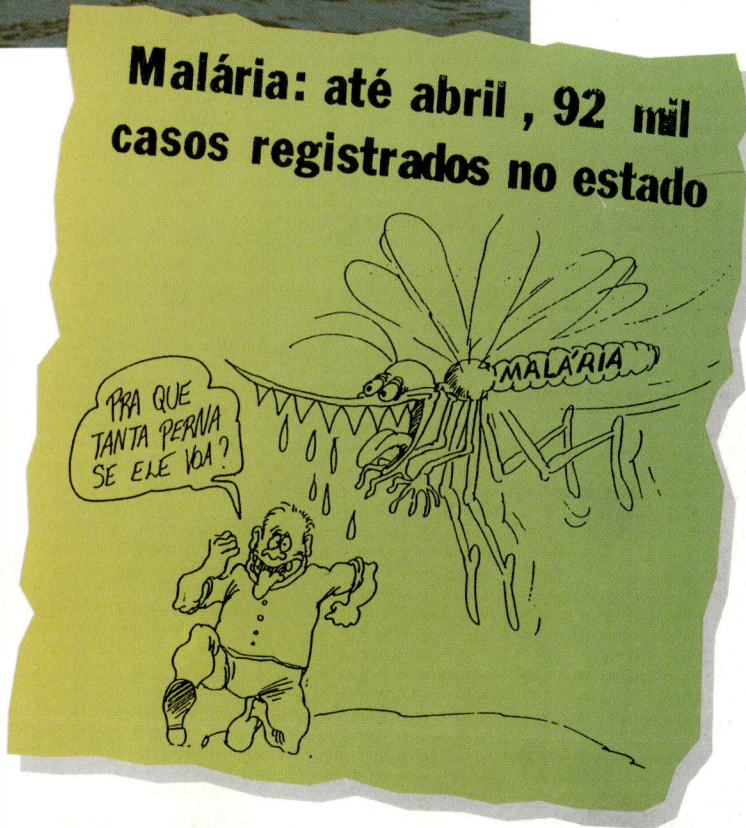

Malária: até abril , 92 mil casos registrados no estado

PRA QUE TANTA PERNA SE ELE VOA?

MALÁRIA

'The gold prospectors leave the land full of holes. Water collects in them. This forms a breeding ground for mosquitos. Everyone is now sick with malaria.'

In the state of Rondonia thousands of people are affected by malaria, which is spread by mosquitos.

'The gold diggers don't have land. If they did they wouldn't invade ours. I also see white men suffering in cities because they don't have a place to live. Everyone has been suffering. This government has not been running the country well enough to give Brazilian people a good life.'

Activity 1

a) Using all the evidence on these pages, explain in words or diagrams how the environment of the Amazon has been damaged by gold mining.

b) How has gold mining affected people?

c) Who do you think Davi Yanomami blames for all the damage caused by gold mining activities? Why?

d) Draw a cartoon to illustrate one of the problems of gold mining in the Amazon.

A city in Brazil

Many people in Brazil have moved from the countryside to the cities. These **migrants** are mainly poor people. They build homes on the edge of the city where there is space, sometimes on land they don't own. These areas are called *favelas* in Brazil. The houses are made out of scrap materials and there is often no water or electricity supply. The houses are far from jobs in the city centre. Sometimes the residents of the *favelas* and the city planners get together to improve these areas.

Source 1

A favela

Source 2

Housing zones in a Brazilian city

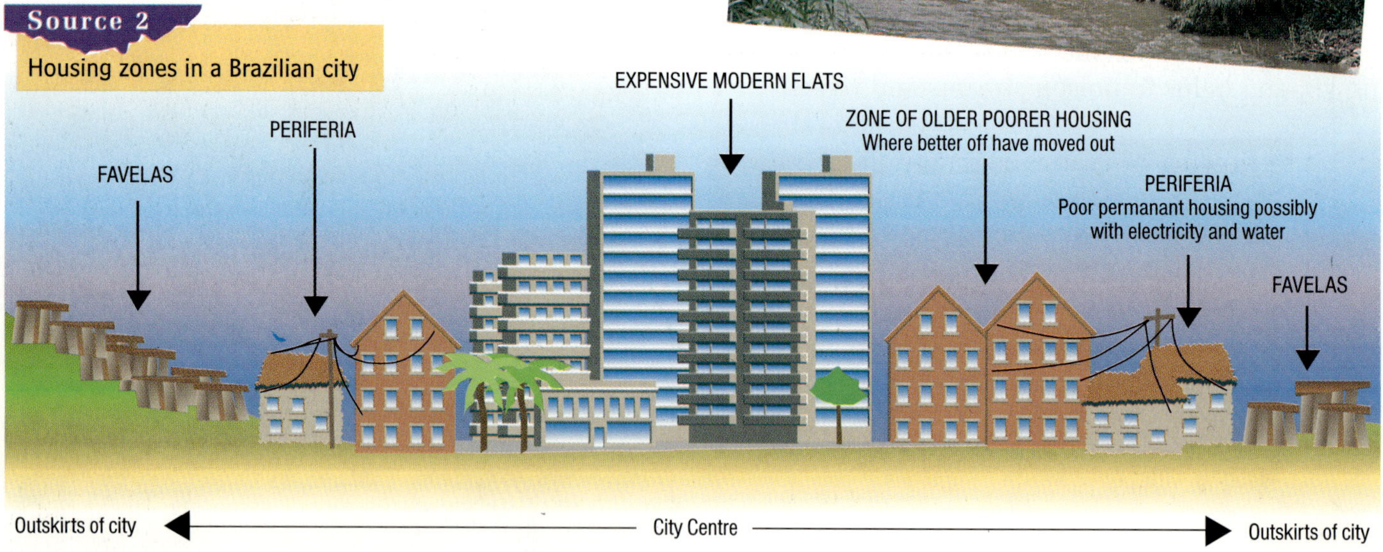

Source 3

Low income housing in Curitiba

Curitiba

Curitiba is a city in the state of Paraná in the south of Brazil. Its population grew very fast from half a million people in 1971 to over one and a half million in 1991. Rapid growth like this can lead to many problems, but Curitiba recently won an environmental prize from the United Nations for planning a good transport system and helping people living in poor parts of the city.

Activity 1

Study Source 2. In which zones of the city do you think Sources 1 and 3 are located? Explain your answer.

The city planners knew the city was growing and gave land to the poor people near the places where new roads were being built, towards the edge of the city. They improved public transport by setting up bus routes serving most areas of the city.

The streets were widened to make special lanes for buses. Curitiba's bus system is so good that fewer people use cars than in other Brazilian cities. There are bus stops every 400 metres, with telephones, newspaper kiosks and post office facilities.

Curitiba's planners also set up the 'Green Market' project. People are given free bus vouchers in exchange for their rubbish. The rubbish is taken to a recycling plant on the edge of the city. This plant provides jobs.

Activity 2

a) Why do you think it is important for people living in the *favelas* to be able to get to the city centre easily?

b) Look at the pattern of Curitiba's bus routes (Source 5).

Which routes are:

i) concentric (linking places in circles around the city centre)?
ii) radial (linking the edge of the city to the centre)?

c) What are the advantages of having facilities at bus stops?

Source 4

A main street in Curitiba

Source 5

Bus routes in Curitiba

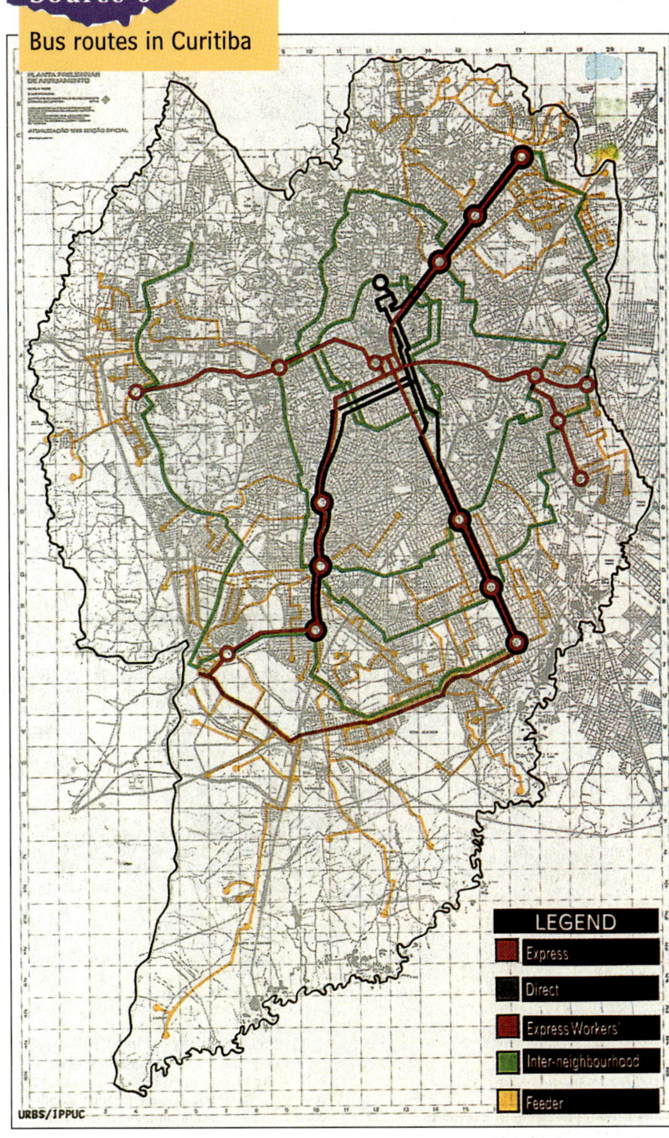

The city planners have helped some of the poorest people of Curitiba and improved the urban environment.

Group Activity

The Mayor of Curitiba wants to be elected again. Work in pairs to decide why the mayor might expect to be re-elected.
Write the speech the Mayor might make about how life has improved for people in Curitiba in the last five years.

People working for change

Since the 1960s, Brazil has developed its industries and tried to make as much money as possible in order to bring about economic growth. It had to borrow money to achieve this growth. As Brazil tries to pay back its loans, it uses up more natural resources and the lives of most of its poor people have not improved.

Source 1

Developed to death

Activity 1

Study Source 1 carefully.

a) Decide which groups of people are winners and losers in Brazil. Look through the pages on Brazil in this book to help you. Make a list of winners and a list of losers.

b) Add one more group of
   i) winners and
   ii) losers.

Change

Some people believe that the only long lasting solutions to Brazil's problems are those which involve ordinary people. Many poor communities are working to change their lives. With the help of organisations from other places they have achieved some success. Sources 2 and 3 are two examples:

Source 2

Arruar and Oxfam

'Maria José Ferreira, a seamstress in Entre a Pulso, draws a map of her neighbourhood for a slum improvement scheme'

In the slum of *Entre a Pulso* in Recife, an organisation called Arruar is helping slum dwellers. The community decides what it wants ... for example open space or community buildings. The money, which comes from OXFAM, pays for a team of architects, engineers and lawyers to help the community. The architects draw up plans, then engineers work on the technical side of building and the lawyers try to get legal ownership of the land for the community.

Source 3

Indian groups and Survival International

Indian people in Brazil have formed organisations to fight for their rights in the Amazon. These include the Organisation of Indian Peoples of the River Envira, the Manitoba Indian Brotherhood and the Alliance of Forest Peoples. Survival International is a worldwide organisation helping Indian groups to stand up for their rights, to decide their own futures and to protect their lives, lands and human rights.

Brazil's future

21st CENTURY GEOGRAPHY

September issue 2010

Group Activity

You will need to work in groups for this activity.

Imagine it is the year 2010. You are a group of writers for a geography magazine for school students called *Twenty-first century geography*.

Your task is to write four articles on Brazil. Each of you must write one article. One must be about the district of *Entre a Pulso* in Recife. Another must be about the Indian people in Brazil. You must decide on topics for the other two articles. You could choose one of the **places** in Brazil covered in this section or one of the **issues**. In your groups you should discuss:

- What things might be better in the year 2010?
- What things might have stayed the same as today or become worse?
- Will your group decide to write the **ideal** future for Brazil in each article or will you write about futures which are most **likely** to happen?

Now write your articles. You can illustrate them if you want to.

Italy

Italy is easy to recognise on a map of Europe because it is a **peninsula** (land surrounded on three sides by water). Source 1 shows Italy's three regions: the North, Centre and South and the main cities. People usually think of Italy as a nation that is mad about soccer, pasta, espresso coffee and opera. This is a **stereotype**, and a closer look at the country will reveal great contrasts. A journey from the north to the south brings dramatic changes in climate, customs, diet and even language. Even though Italy is only slightly larger than the UK, it is a land of great variety. Some of these contrasts will be explored in this unit.

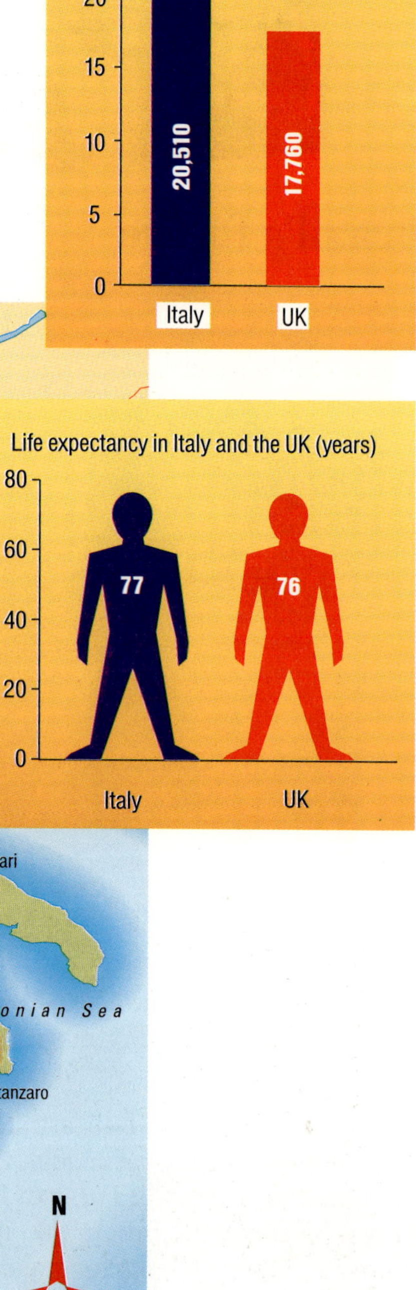

Source 1
Italy

NORTH
Milan
Venice
Turin
Genoa
Adriatic Sea
Florence
CORSICA
Perugia
CENTRE
Rome
Bari
Naples
SOUTH
Tyrrhenian Sea
SARDINIA
Cagliari
Ionian Sea
Catanzaro
0 200 km
Palermo
SICILY
Mediterranean Sea
N

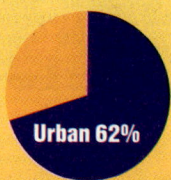

The urban population of Italy and the UK

Urban 62%
Italy

Urban 92%
UK

Activity 1

From city to region

Here is a list of cities in Italy. Use the map in Source 1 to find which region each city is in. The first one has been completed for you:

- Naples is in the south of Italy.
- Rome is in __________________.
- Florence is in __________________.
- Milan is in __________________.
- Perugia is in __________________.
- Genoa is in __________________.

Source 2

Italy and the UK compared

	Italy	UK
Population in millions	57.2	58.4
Area in km^2	294,068	241,595
Density of people per km^2	194	241
% population growth	0.0	0.2
Literacy %	94.4	99

Activity 2

Use an atlas to help you with this activity:

- Name the three main seas surrounding Italy.
- Which countries share a border with Italy? (There are four.)
- Name the two large islands in the sea to the west of Italy. Which country does each one belong to?

Activity 3

Look at the data on Italy and the UK in Sources 1 and 2.

a) Which country has the highest GNP (wealth)?

b) Which country has the largest area?

c) In which country do people live slightly longer?

d) Using all the Sources on these pages write a few sentences comparing Italy and the UK.

Source 3

The Amalfi coastline, south of Naples. Only 60 years ago, the villages along this coastline relied on fishing for work.

Source 4

Turin is a city on the North Italian Plain. It is dominated by factories linked to car production. Fiat (shown here) is the largest, employing 150,000 people.

Landscapes of ice and fire

Source 1

A physical map of Italy

Italy is a country with large mountain ranges (Source 1). These include the Alps (Source 2) and the Apennines which make up about 75 per cent of the total land area. There are islands such as Sicily and Sardinia and several coastal plains. The largest area of lowland is the Po Basin in the north.

The Alps, which spread over several countries apart from Italy are among the highest mountains in Europe. Glaciers have created spectacular scenery over a long period of time. Parts of Italy lie at the edges of continental plates. In the past, movements at the edges of the plates have caused earthquakes and volcanoes.

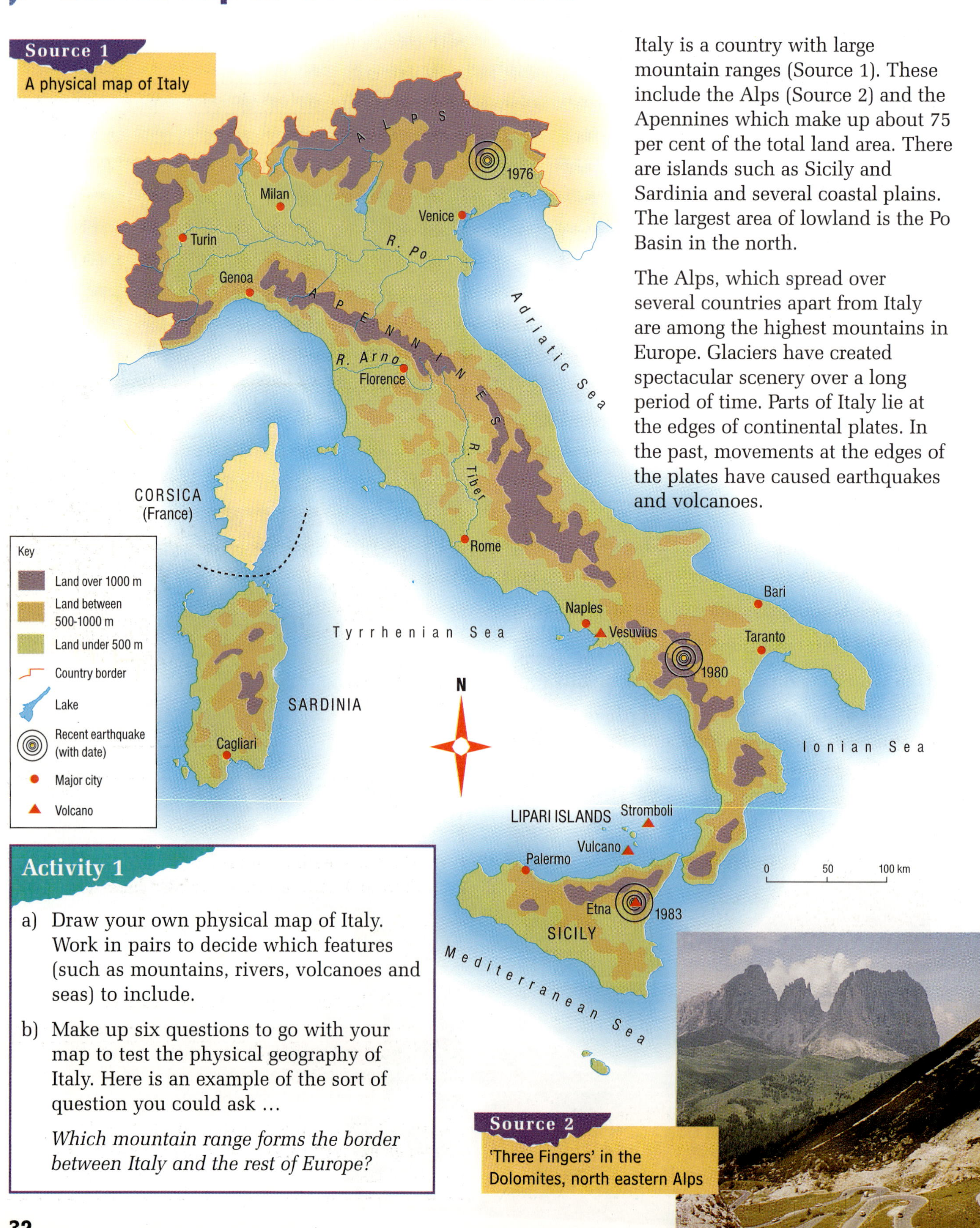

Source 2

'Three Fingers' in the Dolomites, north eastern Alps

Activity 1

a) Draw your own physical map of Italy. Work in pairs to decide which features (such as mountains, rivers, volcanoes and seas) to include.

b) Make up six questions to go with your map to test the physical geography of Italy. Here is an example of the sort of question you could ask …

Which mountain range forms the border between Italy and the rest of Europe?

Earthquakes and volcanoes

An **earthquake** is a violent shaking of the earth's crust caused by the shockwaves which occur when rocks in the earth's crust split (Source 3).

The world's fourth largest earthquake struck Messina in Sicily in 1908, killing 160,000 people. There have been many earthquakes since. The most recent causing loss of life was near Naples in 1980 when 3000 people died.

Italy has Europe's only active **volcanoes**: Etna on Sicily, Vesuvius near Naples (Source 4), Vulcano and Stromboli. Find these volcanoes on the map in Source 1. There are also many extinct volcanoes.

Source 3

How an earthquake happens

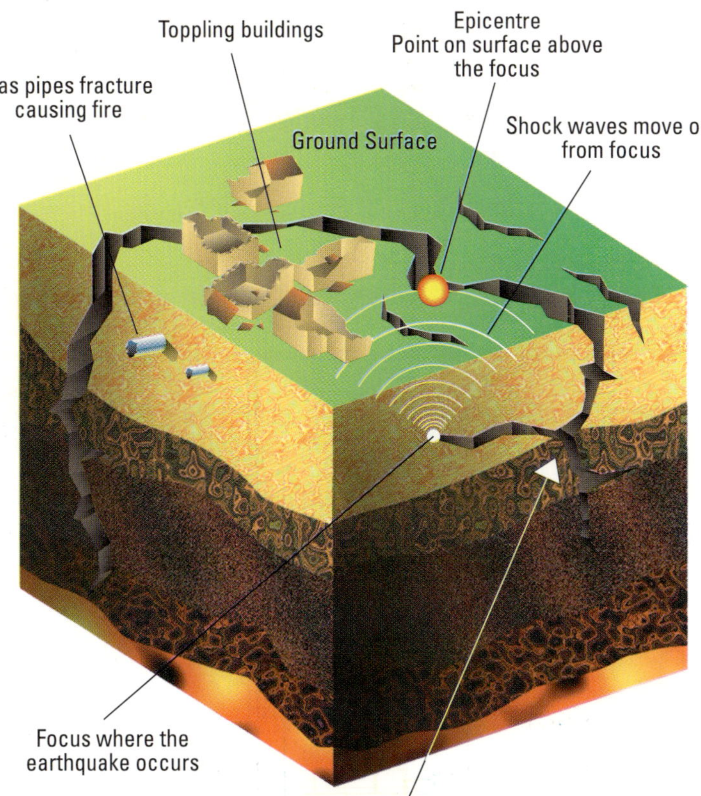

Source 4

Mount Vesuvius, near Naples

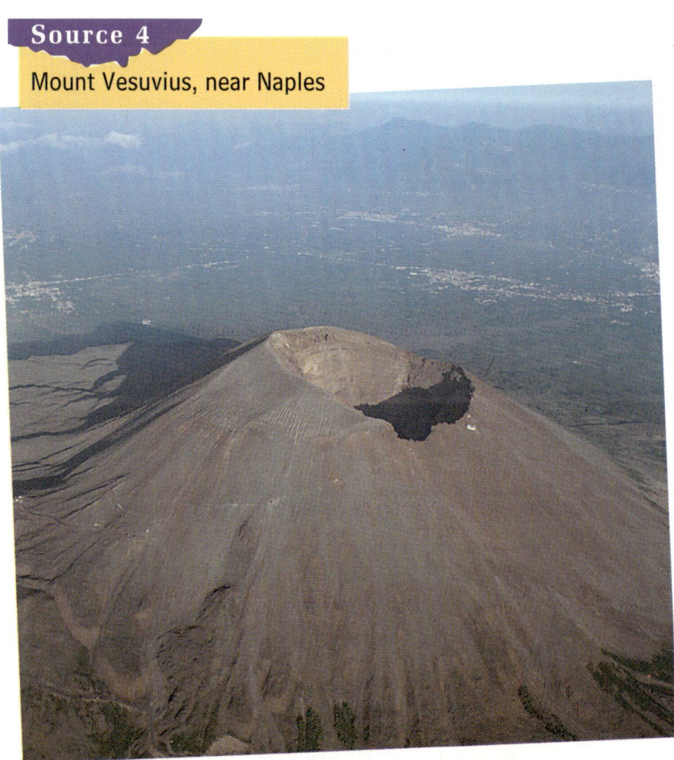

Activity 2

a) Make a sketch of Mount Vesuvius from Source 4. Add a title and these labels:

steep slopes | lava and ash | crater

b) Describe the shape of Mount Vesuvius.

Group Activity

Using Source 3, discuss in small groups the damage an earthquake can cause. Note down your ideas.

Earthquake: a shaking of the earth's crust.

Volcano: a cone-shaped mountain made up of lava and ash, created by eruptions.

Contrasts in climate

Italy's climate changes from north to south because of the country's great length (over 1,000 km). Look at Source 1 carefully. It shows the climate for three towns in Italy. Where would you choose to go skiing or for a sunny summer holiday?

Source 1

The climate of three towns in Italy

Milan (Po Basin)

	J	F	M	A	M	J	J	A	S	O	N	D
Temperature (°C)	30	55	70	95	105	80	70	80	85	23	115	75
Rainfall (mm)	2	4	8	13	18	22	24	23	19	13	7	3

Palermo (Sicily)

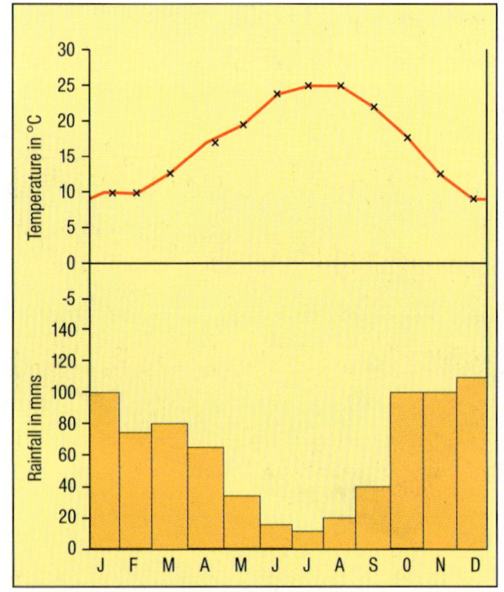

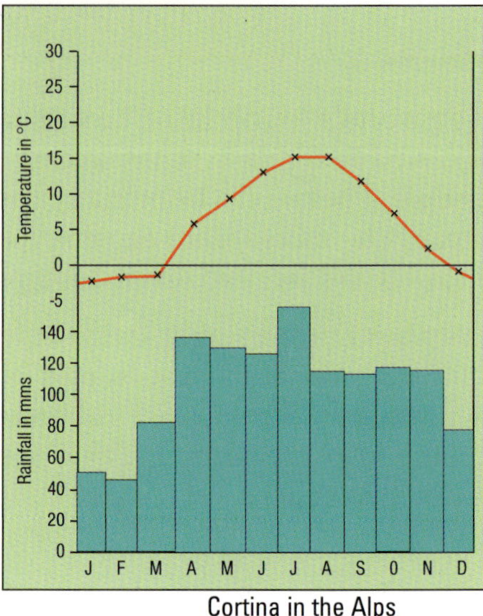

Cortina in the Alps

Activity 1

a) Draw a climate graph for Milan from the data in Source 1. Use the ones already drawn for you as a guide.

b) Match the descriptions below to the climate graphs and identify the three towns of Milan, Cortina and Palermo.

Town 1 has a Mediterranean climate with mild, wet winters and hot, dry summers. The area is popular for tourists seeking holidays in the sun.

Town 2 has an Alpine climate with its cool, damp summers and cold snowy winters, ideal for skiing.

Town 3 has a continental climate with warm, showery summers and cool winters.

c) On an outline map of Italy mark and label the areas of Italy which will have:

- an Alpine climate
- a continental climate
- a Mediterranean climate.

d) Make up some symbols for sunshine, summer showers, snow, skiing and beach holidays. Mark your symbols in the correct places on the map and add a key.

There's no business like snow business!

Study Source 2. Snow is fun for those who enjoy winter sports. The visitors also bring money to the Alpine villages. But the snow can cause problems for people who live in the Alps. They must pay for extra heating, special clothing, snow blowers and avalanche protection.

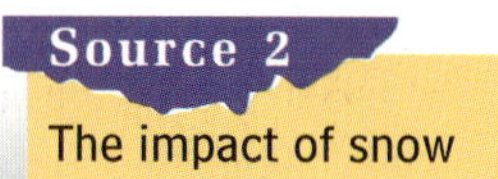

Source 2

The impact of snow

TOWN CUT OFF IN BLIZZARD

FIVE FEARED DEAD IN AVALANCHE

HEAVY SNOW BRINGS DRIVER CHAOS

Minus 10°c-THE BIG FREEZE

Group Activity

Using the text and Source 2, discuss in small groups the advantages and disadvantages of the snow in the Alps. Make two full lists and copy them into your notes.

The avalanche hazard

A mass of snow moving quickly down a mountainside is called an **avalanche**. These can be dangerous as they may reach a speed of 300 km per hour. Avalanches can flatten trees, damage property and kill people and animals.

Avalanche protection can be very expensive. People in the Alps use trees and fences to trap the snow and slow it down (Source 4). They place avalanche shelters over roads and buildings. Avalanche maps and weather forecasts warn skiers and climbers of the dangers.

Source 3

An avalanche hits an Alpine village

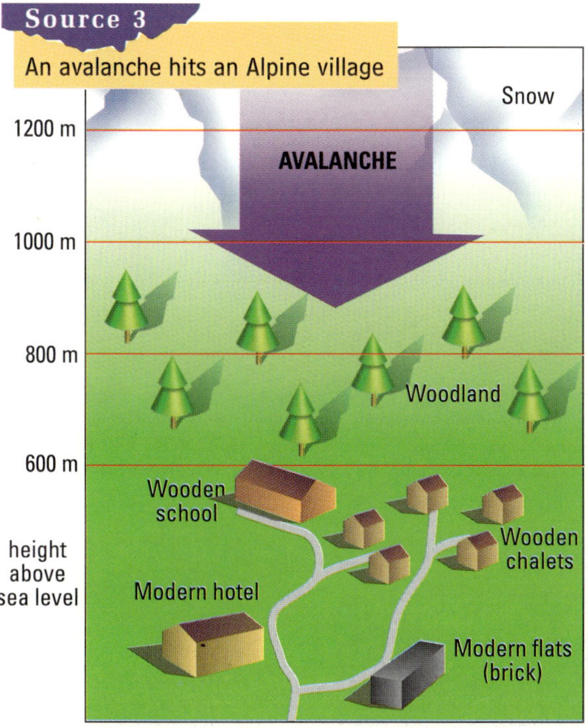

Activity 3

a) Study Source 3. What do you think will happen as the avalanche moves down the hillside and through the village?

b) Make a copy of Source 3 and add three features which would reduce the avalanche hazard. Source 4 provides one clue!

Source 4

Avalanche protection

Living in the Alps

Source 1

Living in the Alps

Some people think of the Alps as an environment which is difficult to live in: the weather may be harsh, especially in winter, and the steep hills make transport difficult. Other people find the Alps beautiful and exciting. Visitors love to ski, walk, rock climb or relax beside the lakes.

Activity 1

Study the Alpine valley illustrated on these two pages (Source 1).

a) Work in pairs and suggest answers to these questions:

- Why do few people live in the Alps?
- Why are the villages, roads and railways on the valley floor?
- Why can Hydro-electric Power (HEP) be produced?
- Why do the farmers take their cattle to the high Alp in summer?

b) Copy and complete the table below by adding some of the types of work found in an Alpine valley:

Primary industry	Secondary industry	Tertiary industry

Public enquiry

The Aosta valley in the Alps in north-west Italy is developing as a winter holiday area. Small villages such as La Thuile (Source 2) are near Mont Blanc and there is plenty of snow in winter.

Developing tourism is not always popular. A **public enquiry** may be held to decide whether tourist development should be allowed to go ahead. The enquiry has a chairperson who listens to evidence given by local people and groups. He or she then makes a decision in favour or against the development.

The farming village in Source 1 could be La Thuile, which is about to hold a public enquiry to decide whether it should develop as a ski resort.

Group Activity

a) Imagine you live in the village and are about to take part in the public enquiry. In small groups, choose one of the following roles:

- a farmer
- a conservationist
- a hotel developer
- an unemployed school leaver

Write a report to present at the enquiry giving your views on how the village should develop.

b) Elect a chairperson who can conduct the enquiry.

c) Hold your enquiry and decide what you think should happen.

d) The village in the picture actually decided to go ahead and develop as a ski resort. What changes do you think this might bring to:

- village life and buildings?
- the availability of jobs?
- the local environment?

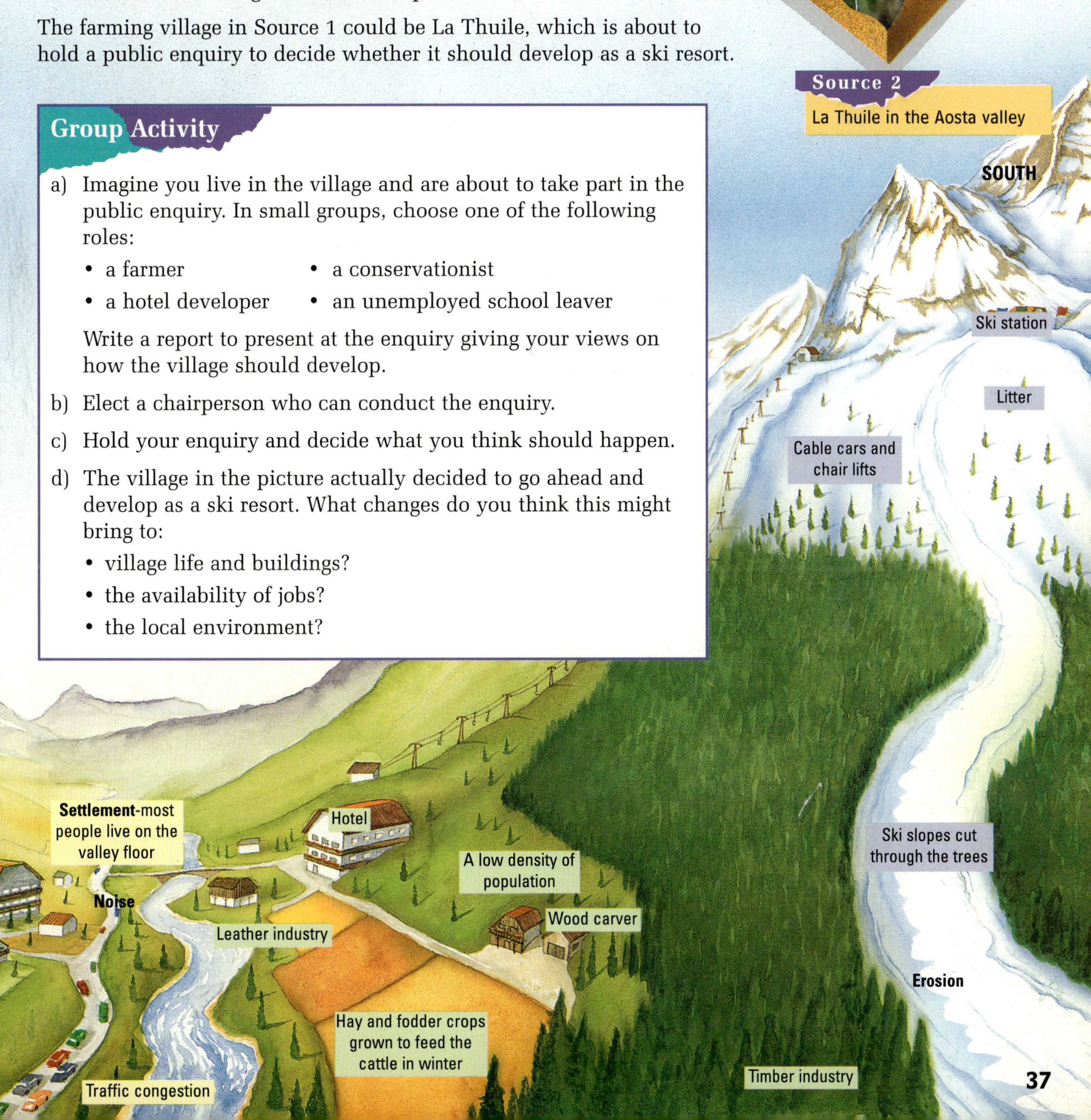

Source 2
La Thuile in the Aosta valley

The North Italian Plain

The North Italian Plain or Po Basin lies between the Alps in the north and the Apennines in the south and is the largest area of lowland in Italy. It is often called the power-house of Italy because it has the best farmland, energy supplies and industries in the country. Three great cities on the plain – Milan, Turin and Genoa – produce most of the country's wealth. Together these form the Italian **'Industrial Triangle'** (see Source 1).

Source 1
The North Italian Plain

Key
Wine
Rice
Maize
Wheat for pasta
Tomatoes
Fruit growing
Beef & dairy cattle
Gas & oil
Cheap HEP
Road Passes/Tunnels
Simplon Pass
St Gothard Pass
ALPS
Brenner Pass
Snowmelt for irrigation water
Large market in cities
Milan
Verona
Venice
Turin
Industrial Triangle
Lowland with fertile soils
River Po
Po Delta
Rain all year
APENNINES
Genoa
OIL, IMPORTS & EXPORTS
Bologna
OIL, IMPORTS & EXPORTS

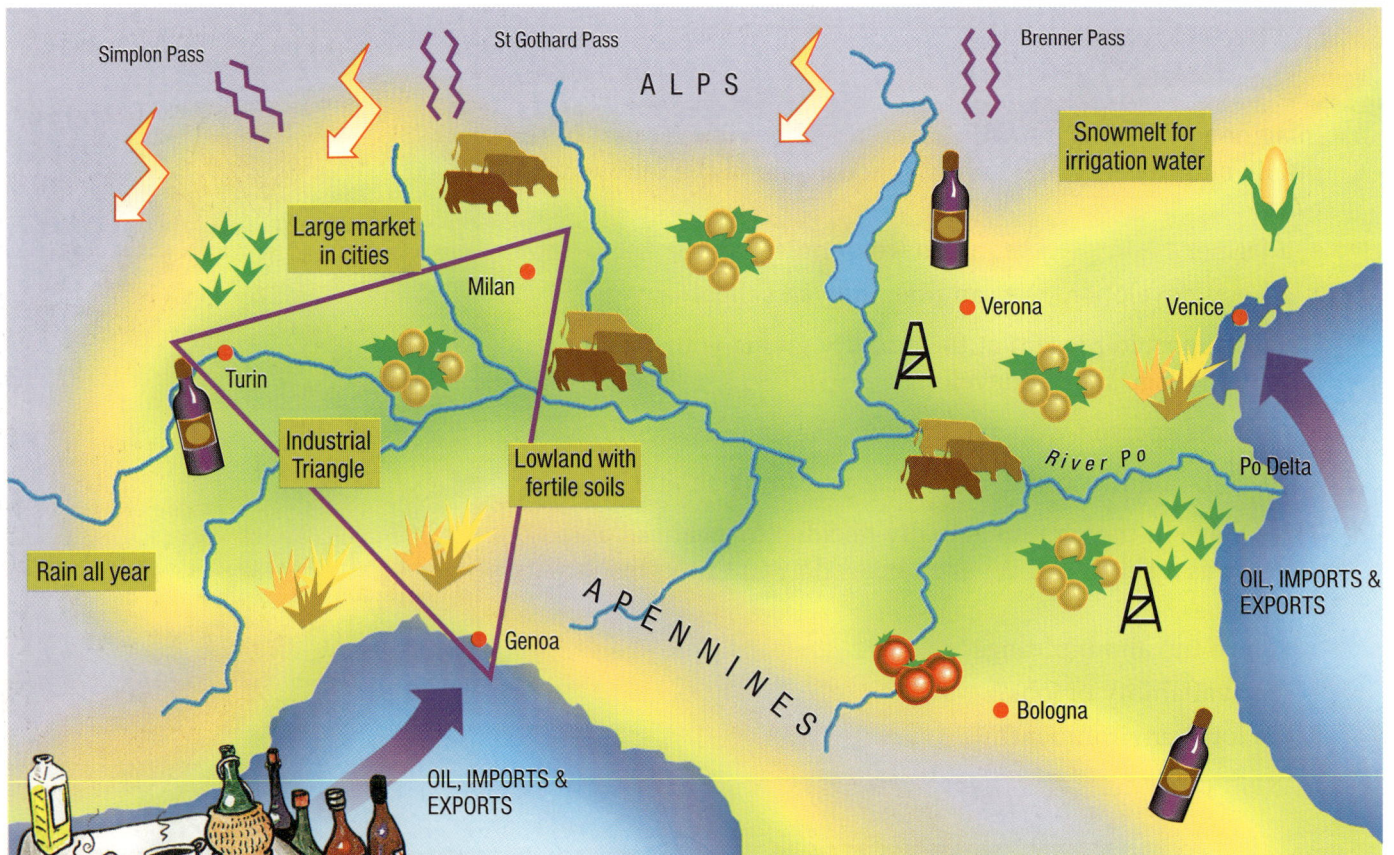

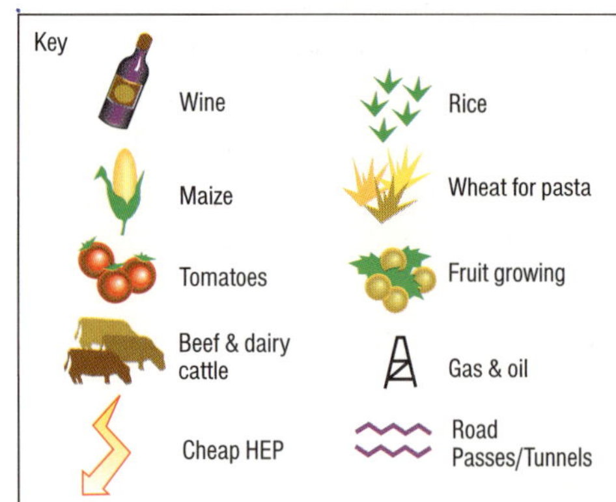

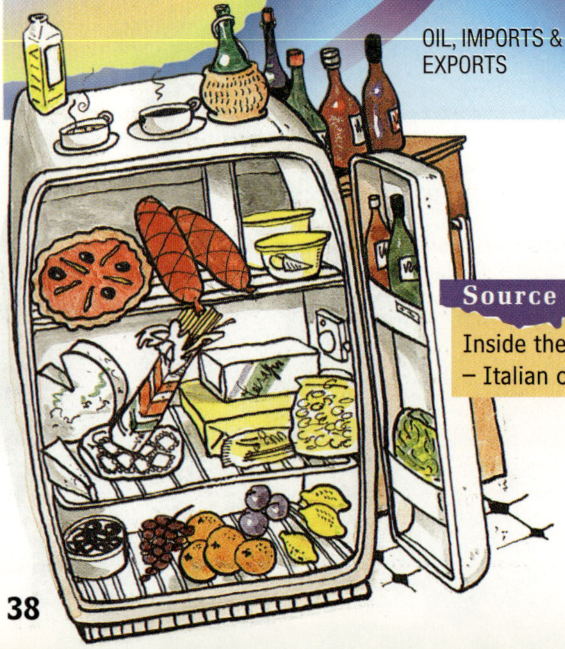

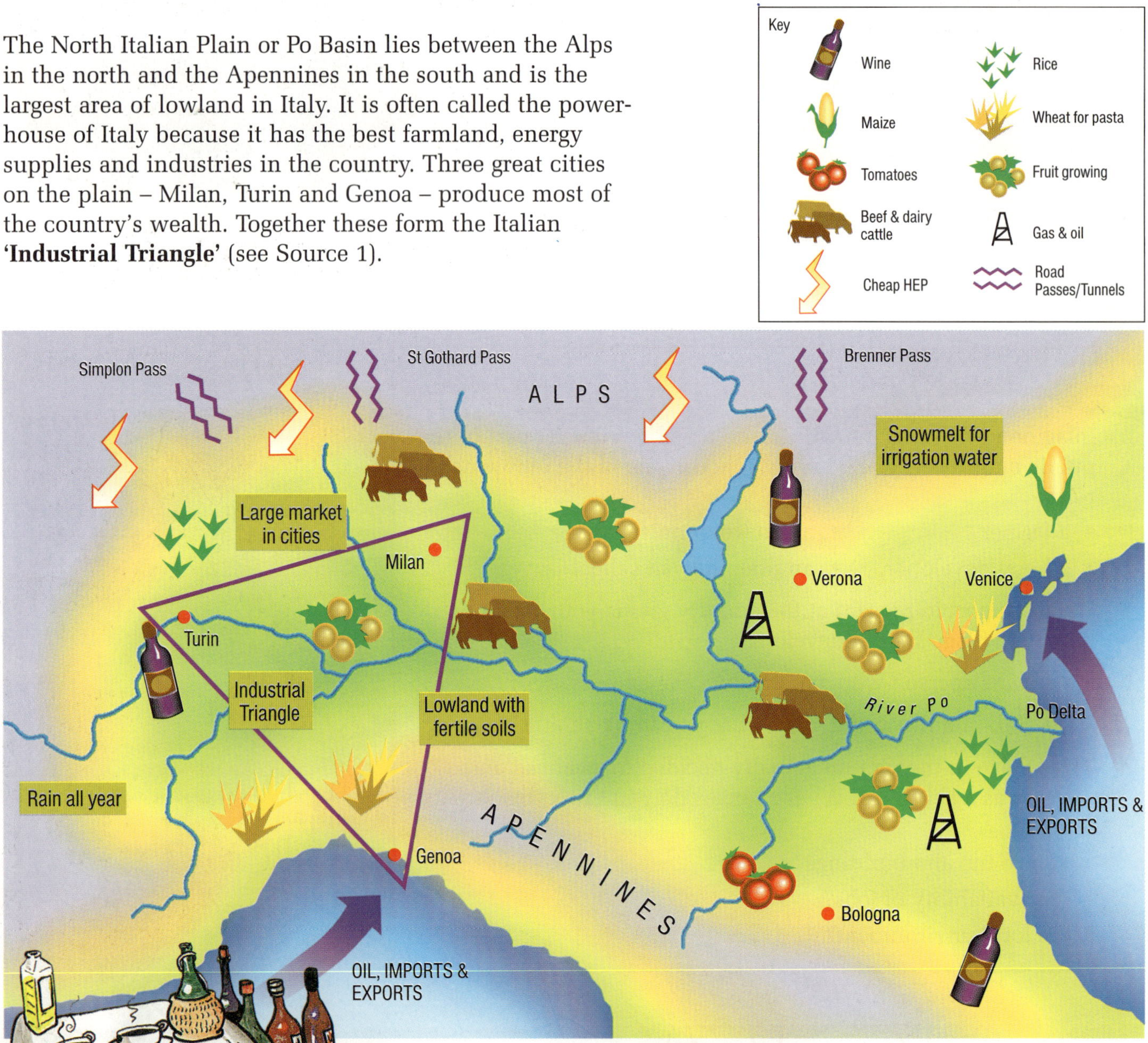

Source 2
Inside the fridge – Italian cuisine

Activity 1

a) Using Source 1 and what you have read, list the reasons why the North Italian Plain is so prosperous.

b) Study Sources 1 and 2. Design a typical Italian menu which uses the farm produce grown in the region. Try to include a starter, main course and pudding as well as something to drink.

The River Po

The River Po is joined by many smaller rivers, or **tributaries**, as it meanders eastwards into the Adriatic Sea. At its mouth it forms a **delta** south of Venice (see Source 1). The newspaper article in Source 3 describes some of the pollution problems in the River Po and the Adriatic Sea.

Source 3

The polluted River Po

The polluted Po

In the summer months thousands of tourists visit Italy's Adriatic coast, the invasion by black algae in 1989 now forgotten. But water pollution in the Adriatic is still a serious problem.

The main source of the pollution is the river Po which passes through Italy's largest industrial and heavily farmed regions. The main cities of Turin and Milan have used the Po as their dustbin, dumping sewage, industrial wastes and cooling water. The farmers have increased their use of pesticides, fertilisers and weedkillers which are washed out of the soil and seep into underground water-stores and streams. This has even affected the drinking water, 70 per cent of which comes from underground sources. Wastes from pig farming and dairy cows also pollute the waters.

Italy claims the pollution is bad but not as bad as in the River Rhine, and a new authority has been set up to prepare a plan for the Po. They are considering reducing farmers' use of chemicals as one way of tackling the problem.

Fertiliser: plant foods added to the soil to increase crop growth.

Meander: a bend in a river.

Tributary: a small river flowing into a large river.

Activity 2

Read the newspaper article in Source 3.

a) Copy and complete the flow diagram below to show how the Adriatic Sea is being polluted. Use these words to fill in the boxes:

Animal wastes | Adriatic Sea | Fertiliser | Sewage

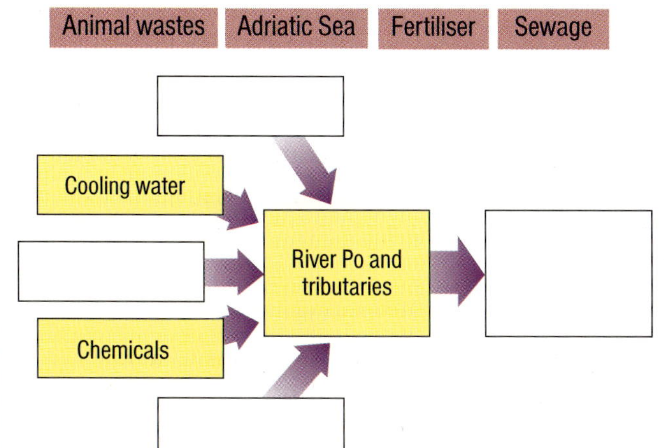

Illustrate your diagram with pictures.

b) In pairs discuss how the pollution could be reduced. You may like to investigate how pollution has been reduced in a local river or the river Thames. Write a report to present to the Po Authority.

Aliano, a village in Southern Italy

Paolo in Source 1 lives in Aliano, a small village in the Apennines in Southern Italy. His English teacher has made contact with a school in the UK and he has written his first letter (Source 2) to his new penfriends.

Source 1

Paolo

Aliano, July 1995

Dear Richard and Jane,

In my first letter to you I hope to tell you about where I live and the life I lead.

Aliano is a small village in Southern Italy. The only way to reach the village is along winding roads. The village lies on a hill between two rivers.

The weather has been very hot, over 30°C most days and it hasn't rained for a month. The rivers have dried up. The slopes are very steep down to the rivers. The land is poor and little grows in the thin soils. The heavy rains in winter wash the soil away and the rivers flood.

Close to the village there are vines and olives growing. We also grow a little wheat to make pasta. Further away the land is used to graze sheep and goats but some is too steep and rocky to use at all.

I live in an old house in the village and we are farmers. We eat quite a lot of the food that we grow and we are beginning to plant lemon trees on our land because they fetch a higher price at market. We want to buy a new tractor with the extra money. We are poorer than the people who work in factories in Milan and Turin.

I go to school in the next village and help out on the farm at night and at weekends. The village is very quiet and the farm is hard work. When I am older I want to move to Milan in Northern Italy where I can get a job in a factory.

Please write soon and tell me about yourselves.

Paolo.

Source 2

A letter from Paolo to his penfriends in the UK

Activity 1

Read the letter (Source 2) carefully and study the pictures and maps on page 41. Then:

a) Describe where Aliano is in Italy.

b) List the problems of Aliano linked to: (i) the climate, and (ii) the land.

c) Either: Write a letter back to Paolo saying how your way of life and environment is different.

Or: Draw a series of pictures which show what life is like in Aliano.

Source 3

The Village of Aliano

Land-use at Aliano

Source 4 shows the plan of Aliano that Paolo sent to his penfriends in Britain. The land around the village is used for farming. Some of the land is for grazing animals but the land nearest the village grows crops such as vines and olives. Wheat is grown in winter when there is more rain. In the summer some land close to the river is **irrigated**.

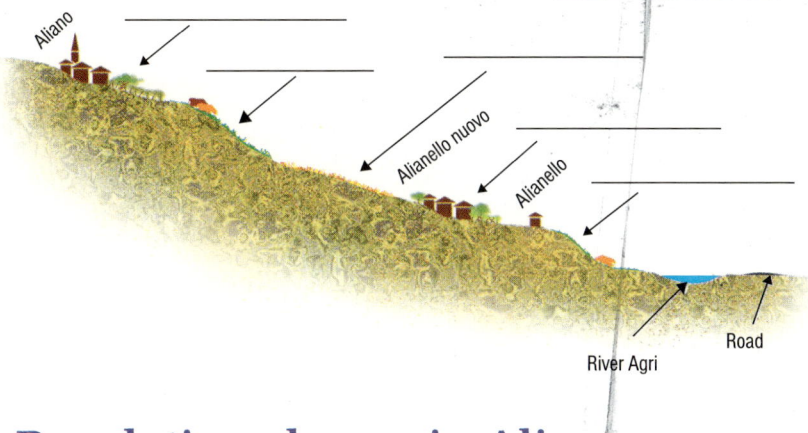

Source 4

Land use in Aliano

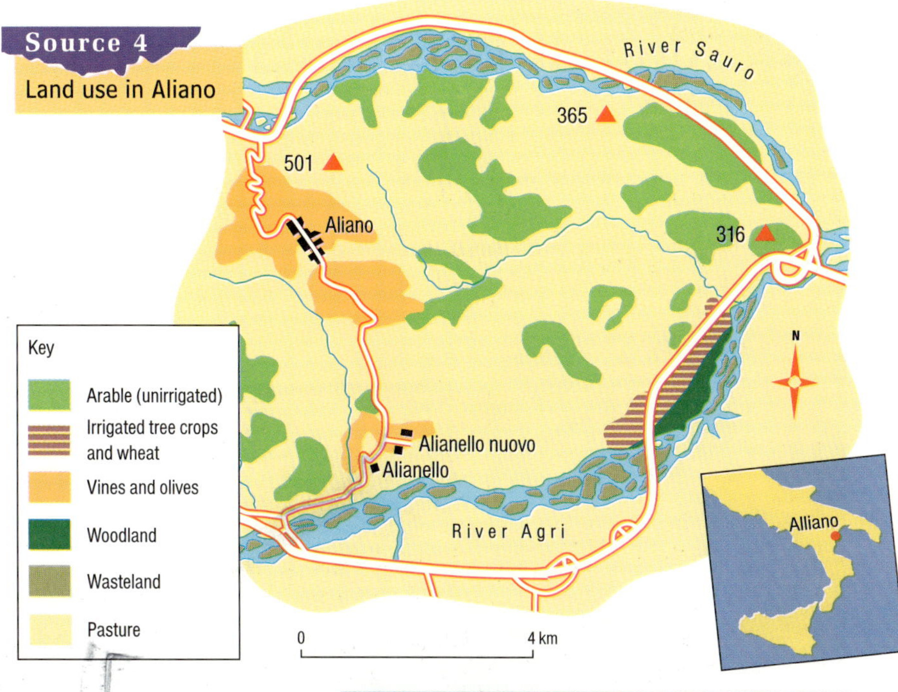

Source 5

A section diagram showing land use from the River Agri to Aliano

Aliano

Alianello nuovo

Alianello

River Agri

Road

Activity 2

Imagine you are walking along the winding road from the River Agri to Aliano. On a copy of the section diagram in Source 5, label the different land uses you would pass.

Population change in Aliano

Like many other young people in Aliano, Paolo wants to move away. This is called **out-migration**. Paolo wants to get away from the harsh life and poverty of the south. These are called **push factors**. He would like to go to Milan where there are better-paid jobs and a higher standard of living. These are called **pull factors**. Source 6 shows what has happened to the population of Aliano since 1951.

Source 6

Population figures for Aliano

Date	Births	Deaths	Natural change	Net migration	Total population
1951	63	37	+26	-27	2288
1960	54	15	+39	-34	2204
1970	29	11	+18	-63	1835
1980	17	16	+1	-27	1714
1987	10	15	-5	-29	1600

Activity 3

a) What has happened since 1951 to:
   i) the number of births in Aliano?
   ii) natural change in population?

b) Plot the figures for total population on a line graph. Describe what your graph shows.

c) Use this equation to find out in which years Aliano's population went up or down – take care with the minus signs!

Natural change + Net migration = Population change

Regional contrasts: North v South

In Italy there is a **north-south divide**. The people in the north are much richer than the people in the south. Source 1 compares two regions, Lombardy in the north where Milan is located, and Basilicata in the south where the village of Aliano is located.

Lombardy Fact File . . .

Employment %

Industry 43.3
Services 53.2
Farming 3.5

LOMBARDY
Milan

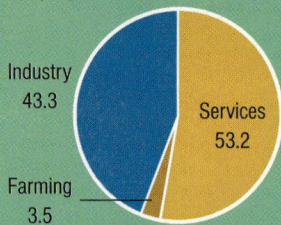

Population	8.9 million
Population density people per km^2	373
Birth rate/1000	8.5
Death rate/1000	9.3
Unemployment %	5.8
Persons per car	2.4
Literacy rate %	99.6
Income per person (million lire)	Over 2500
% Houses with no bath	7

Basilicata Fact File . . .

Employment %

Industry 25.9
Services 52.3
Farming 22.3

BASILICATA
Aliano

Population	616,000
Population density people per km^2	62
Birth rate/1000	10.6
Death rate/1000	8.5
Unemployment %	21.4
Persons per car	4.0
Literacy rate %	91.8
Income per person (million lire)	below 1600
% Houses with no bath	30

Activity 1

a) In small groups discuss the information shown in the fact files. Check that you understand what the figures mean. Try to explain how they show that the north is richer than the south.

b) Copy and complete the sentences below by choosing the correct word from inside each bracket.

In the north, Lombardy has a (*high/low*) population density. The birth rate is (*higher/lower*) than the death rate so the population is (*falling/rising*). In Basilicata the birth rate is (*higher/lower*) than the death rate.

In Basilicata a (*higher/lower*) percentage of people work in farming than in Lombardy, and unemployment is about (*four times/six times*) higher. Fewer people own cars, housing is much (*worse/better*) and a (*higher/lower*) percentage of people can read and write. The people of Basilicata also earn (*more/less*) money than those in Lombardy.

c) Using Source 1 draw some more graphs or pictograms to show the figures for population, income and the percentage of houses with no bath. Label each one correctly.

Developing the south

In 1950, the Italian Government set up the *Cassa Per Il Mezzogiorno* or 'Fund for the South'. The money for this came from the Italian Government and later, the European Union (EU). The money was to be used to improve the south.

At first, the money was spent improving the farming in villages like Aliano (see Source 2). Peasant farmers were offered pensions to retire. Their small farms were joined together to form larger farms. High-value crops such as lemons and tomatoes were planted. There were new irrigation schemes and tractors. Services such as electricity and water were improved, and new schools and hospitals built.

• A Typical Village in the 1950's •

- New Roads
- Draing marsh
- Tree planting to stop erosion
- Modern machinery
- New wheat seeds + modern services eg vines
- Shops, Banks
- Telephones, electricity
- Irrigation
- New crops eg tomatoes, citrus fruits

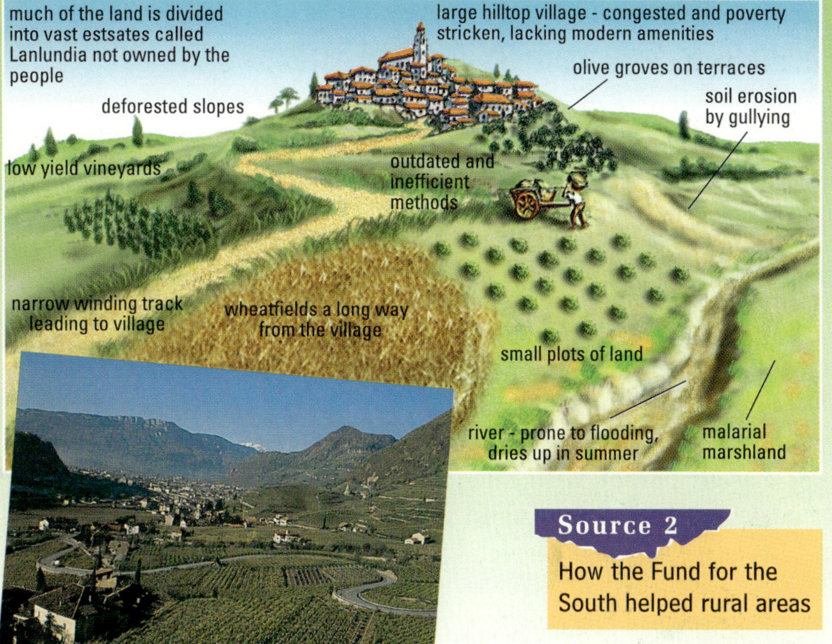

Source 2
How the Fund for the South helped rural areas

Developing industry

From 1957, the *Cassa per Il Mezzogiorno* began to give grants to industry and to build motorways like the *Autostrada del Sole* (Source 3). Fiat built a factory at Palermo in Sicily and a large steelworks was sited at Taranto. Since 1984 a new organisation has been formed to promote tourism.

A happy ending?

Life has improved in villages like Aliano but the south is still one of the poorest regions of Europe. The North-South divide is still as great as it was in 1950 and much of the wealth of the south still comes from outside the region, from grants or money sent home by migrant workers.

Source 3
The Autostrada del Sole, which runs from Milan to Reggio at the toe of Italy

Activity 2

a) Read the text on these pages carefully. Copy the table below and put the following statements into the correct box in the table to show how the south of Italy has improved:

steelworks at Taranto
older farmers retire
tourism growing
new irrigation schemes
Fiat factory at Palermo
lemons grown
electricity
new schools

From 1950	From 1957	From 1984

b) Draw a sketch of Source 3 and add the following labels:

motorway	Apennines
hill-top village	scrub
bare	limestone

c) How do you think the new motorway helps the south of Italy?

Volcanoes: Hazard or blessing?

Volcanoes: the hazard

Heat and pressure (Source 1) often cause rocks deep in the earth's crust to melt. If the resulting **molten rock** finds its way to the surface through cracks in the earth's crust, a volcanic eruption may occur (Source 1). During an eruption, **lava** bursts out of the top of the volcano. Each time lava erupts from the vent another layer of ash and lava is added to the volcano. This builds up a cone-shaped mountain. When a volcano erupts there are many dangers. It produces molten rock or lava along with huge ash clouds, explosions and mud flows.

Source 1

How a volcano erupts

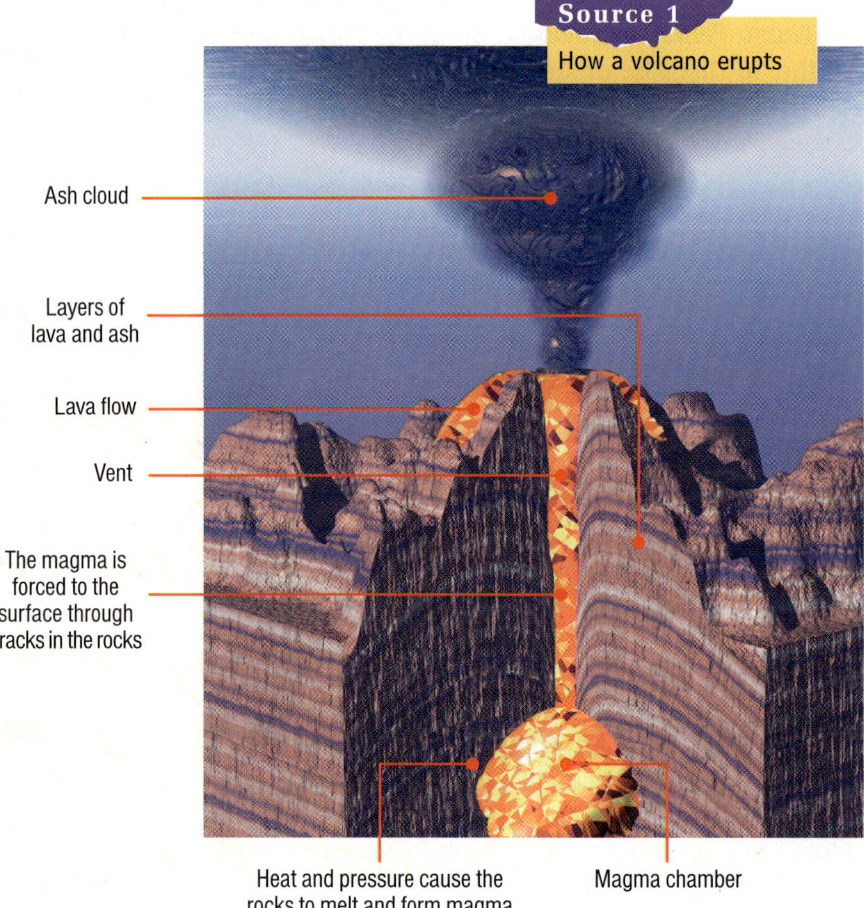

Activity 1

Using Source 1 and the text, explain in your own words how a volcano erupts.

Source 2

Mount Etna erupts

Mount Etna erupts

In recent years, the volcano Mount Etna on Sicily has erupted several times. In March 1983 there were several small earthquakes and the volcano showed signs that it would erupt again. Then, at the end of March a crack appeared and lava started to spill down the sides of the volcano (Source 2). The lava flow was 500 metres wide, 10 to 15 metres high and grew at about 1km per day.

Activity 2

Imagine you are a reporter on Sicily during the eruption. Write a newspaper article describing what happens during the eruption. Include some imagined interviews with local people. Alternatively, you could write a short play about the eruption.

Could the lava be stopped?

In 1983, the Government of Sicily tried to divert the lava flows from Mount Etna away from the threatened villages (Source 3). It used explosives to blast a large channel into which the lava could be re-directed. The scheme cost £3 million but only 20 per cent of the lava went into the channel. The villages of Rocca and Regaina were saved when the lava cooled and came to a halt on its own, before it reached them.

Activity 3

Using Source 3, describe in your own words how the villages of Rocca and Regaina were saved from the lava flows.

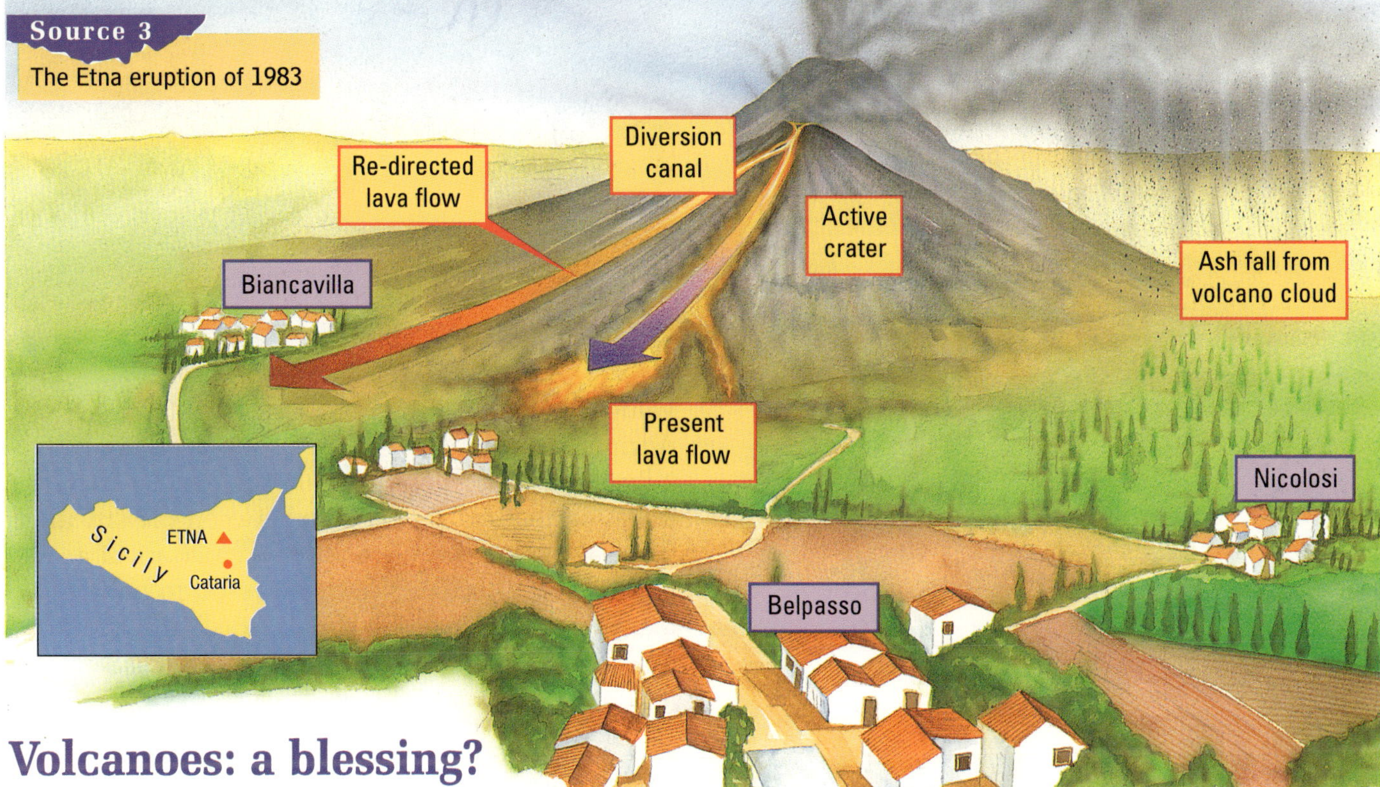

Source 3
The Etna eruption of 1983

Volcanoes: a blessing?

Sicily is a mountainous island. The rocks are mostly limestone and are covered with thin stony soils. There are few rivers and the island has a water shortage. Mount Etna is 3210 metres high and always has snow on the top.

The slopes of Mount Etna are covered in a rich, fertile volcanic soil shich is useful for growing vines and fruit trees, especially lemons and oranges (Source 4). The area is also popular with tourists. There are many hotels, souvenir shops and restaurants located close to the volcano.

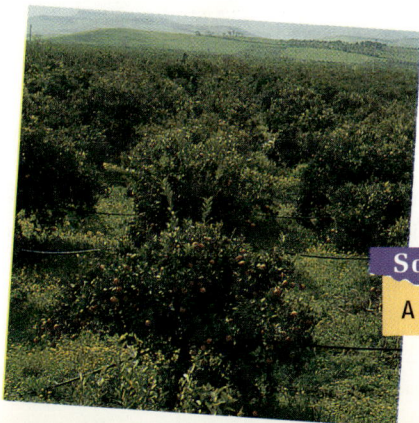

Source 4
A citrus grove on Sicily

Group Activity

a) In pairs discuss the advantages and disadvantages of a plan to move all the local villagers away from Mount Etna. Record your results in a table like the one below.

Advantages of living near Etna	Disadvantages of living near Etna

b) Design your own souvenir which could be sold in one of the shops close to Mount Etna.

Venice

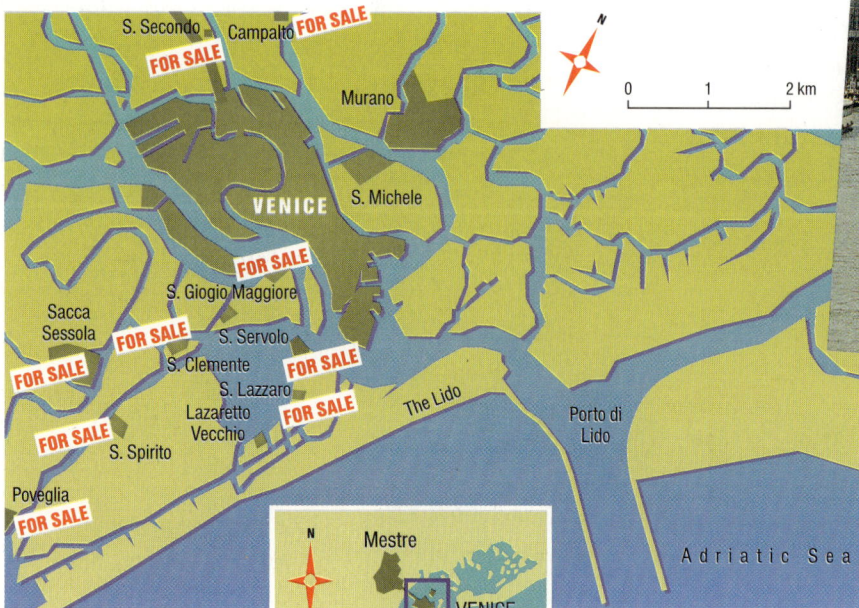

Source 1

Venice

Source 2

Along the Grand Canal

Venice is located at the northern end of the Adriatic Sea (Source 1). The city covers about 2 km^2 and is built on over 100 islands. There is a huge sandbar called the Lido between the city and the sea. Venice was once the headquarters of a powerful empire. Its wealth was used to build many fine buildings (Source 2) filled with art treasures. These, along with the city's canals attract millions of visitors each year.

There are few roads in Venice. Canals separate the islands. The easiest way to travel is by boat. Source 2 shows the famous *gondolas* and *vaporettas*, or buses. Even the rubbish goes by boat (Source 3) as well as the emergency services.

Activity 1

a) Study the text and Sources on this page. Decide which of the statements below are true, and copy them down:
   - Venice is north of the Po Delta.
   - It covers about 20 km^2.
   - It lies at the head of the Adriatic Sea.
   - It is built on many islands separated by canals.
   - The Lido is a sandbar.

b) Using reference books or an encyclopaedia (perhaps on CD-ROM) find out four other facts about Venice. Here are some ideas … What is Venice's population? What are its main industries? Can you find out the names of any famous buildings or people?

Source 3

Moving the rubbish Venice style

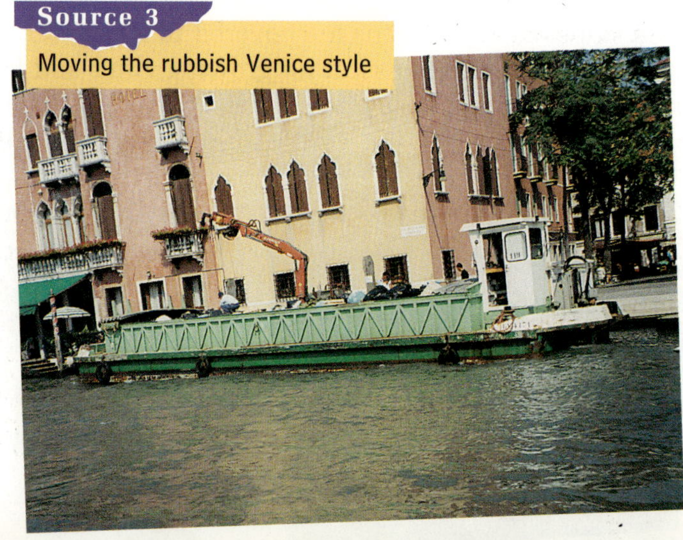

Venice in Peril

Many buildings in Venice are rotting away with rising damp and acid rain pollution. People have abandoned ground floor rooms because of flooding. The authorities cannot afford all of the work to be done. Venice in Peril is an international campaign to raise funds to help. In addition, some of the islands in the lagoon are being sold (Source 4) to raise the money needed for the repairs.

Activity 2

a) Study Source 4 and the text.

i) Why are islands like Poveglia being sold?

ii) Imagine you bought one of islands. Draw your own imaginary island showing how you would develop it.

b) Study Source 5, which outlines the city's main problems and solutions (all jumbled up). In small groups make a list of the problems of Venice, and match the solutions to each problem.

FOR SALE

POVEGLIA

Poveglia is an ex-hospital, set in 22 lush acres; it is also one of the largest islands.

Club Mediterranée has threatened to develop an up-market Butlin's on the site.

Even though a rent of as little as £100 a week has been mentioned, the development costs will be crippling. In 1985 these were estimated to be in the region of £15 million – this has now risen to well over £25 million.

Source 4

Going, going, gone!

Source 5

The problems and solutions

1 billion lira for a sea barrier
STOP WATER PUMPS
RISING DAMP
Close the oil refineries
CLOSED
1992 serious floods hit Venice.
Crumbling buildings
crumble crumble
Population falls 175,000 in 1995 65,000 in 1987
Acid rain rots St Marks.
Build new foundations
Attract new industry
New sewage system
Venice is sinking
1989 Black algae chokes Venice

Acid Rain: a cocktail of chemicals in rain which is acid and corrodes buildings.

Delta: a piece of land built out into the sea at a river's mouth.

Lido: the sand bar near Venice which separates the lagoon from the Adriatic Sea.

The Migration Game

Many people have migrated away from southern Italy to seek employment and a better standard of living. The **migration** is usually done in stages or steps; from rural villages to small cities, from small cities to larger cities and finally from Italy's largest cities to other countries.

Imagine you are a villager living in the less-developed southern region of Italy. You want to find work and good housing in a town outside your village. Play the Migration Game …

Rules of the game

a) Set a time limit for the game (say 30 minutes).

b) Throw a six to start.

c) Record how many moves it takes you to leave each place.

d) If you have a copy of the gameboard, shade in each square that you land on.

e) Write down your migration pattern.

When the time is up, compare your migration pattern with other members of the class. How is your pattern different?

Write a brief account of your pattern of migration and show that you understand **stepped migration**.

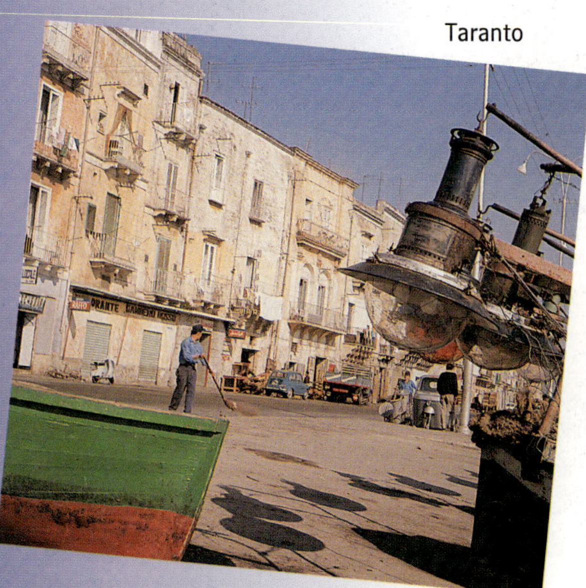

Taranto

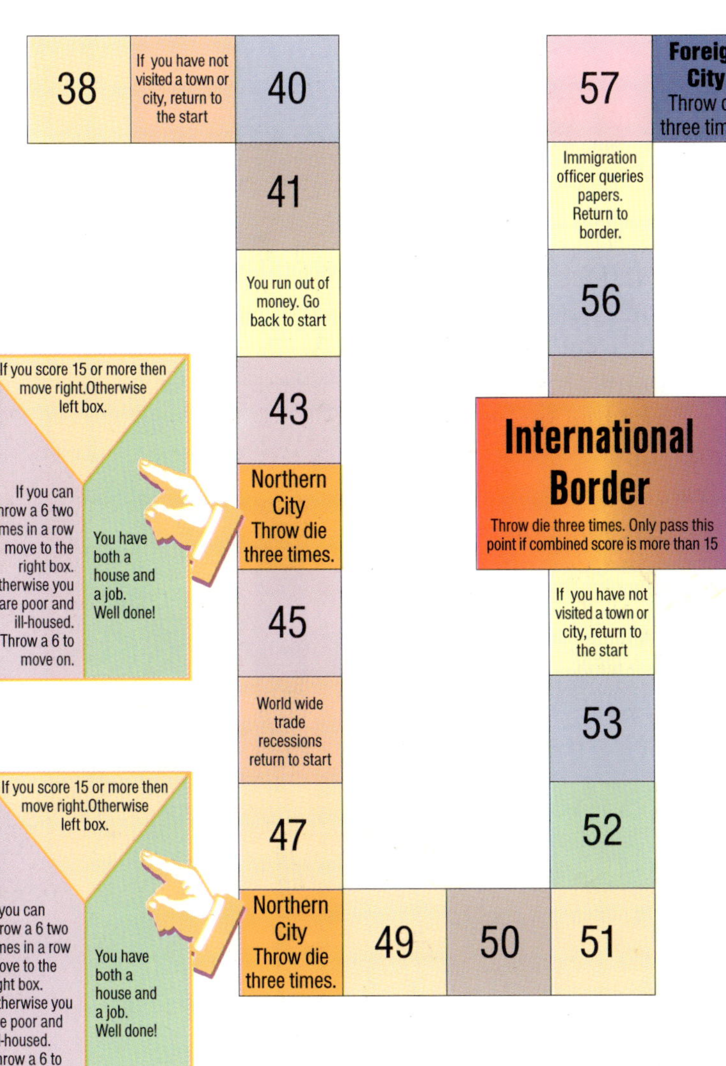
38
If you have not visited a town or city, return to the start
40
41
You run out of money. Go back to start
43
Northern City Throw die three times.
45
World wide trade recessions return to start
47
Northern City Throw die three times.
49
50
51
52
53
If you have not visited a town or city, return to the start
International Border
Throw die three times. Only pass this point if combined score is more than 15
56
Immigration officer queries papers. Return to border.
57
Foreign City Throw die three times.
If you score 15 or more then move right.Otherwise left box.
If you can throw a 6 two times in a row move to the right box. Otherwise you are poor and ill-housed. Throw a 6 to move on.
You have both a house and a job. Well done!
If you score 15 or more then move right.Otherwise left box.
If you can throw a 6 two times in a row move to the right box. Otherwise you are poor and ill-housed. Throw a 6 to move on.
You have both a house and a job. Well done!

If your score is 17 or 18, go to the upper box.

You have a house and a job. Send for your relatives.

You are a poor migrant in a ghetto. If you throw a 6 three times in a row before the end of the game, move to the upper box.

Turin or Milan | New York

New York

The Opera House, Milan

Unit review: Tops and tails

Match each word or phrase with the correct definition:

Alpine climate	The movement of people
Avalanche	A volcano in the Lipari Islands
Company town	Hot, dry summers, mild wet winters
Earthquake	Cone-shaped mountain of lava
HEP	Poor south v rich north of Italy
Industrial triangle	A town based upon one industry
Mediterranean climate	Hydro-electric power
Migration	Snowy winters and cool summers
North-South divide	The area drained by the River Po
Po Basin	The seasonal movement of animals
Stromboli	Wealthy region of Milan, Turin, Genoa
Transhumance	A shaking of the earth's crust
Volcano	A mass of snow moving rapidly downhill

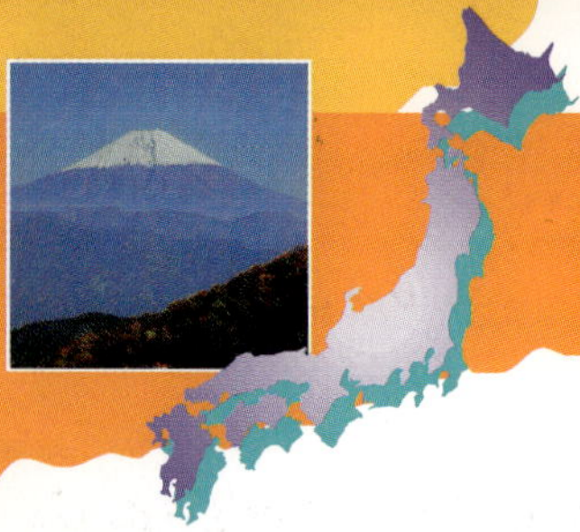

Japan

'Made in Japan'. You see these words on products at home and in shops and offices. But what is Japan really like?

Japan is made up of four main islands. Over 75 per cent of the land area is covered by mountains. This means that much of the population is squeezed into the lowland areas. As a result these are very crowded, like the region between Tokyo and Osaka. One image of Japan is of a modern, bustling country but Japanese people are proud of their traditions too. Some still live in wooden homes and enjoy watching sports like Sumo wrestling. These are just some of the contrasts explored in this unit.

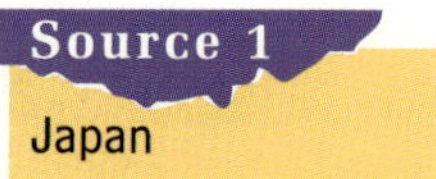

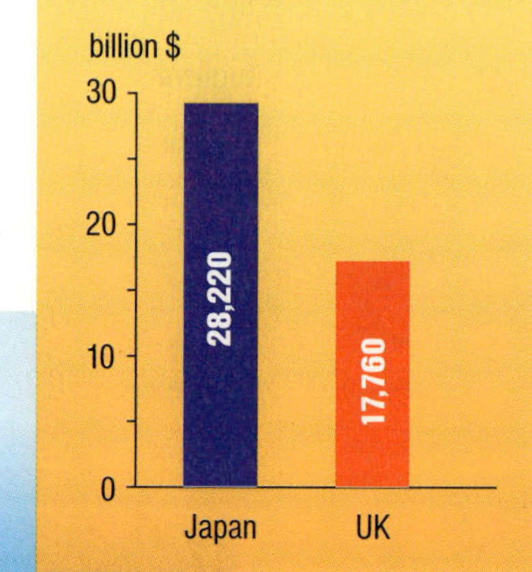

Source 1

Japan

Gross National Product (GNP) of Japan and the UK
billion $
30
20
10
0
28,220
17,760
Japan
UK

N
The urban population of Japan and the UK
Urban 77%
Japan
Urban 92%
UK
Sea of Japan
HOKKAIDO
Sapporo
Aomori
Niigata
HONSHU
Tokyo
Yokohama
Mt. Fuji
Nagoya
Kyoto
Osaka
Hiroshima
Kitakyushu
Inland Sea
SHIKOKU
KYUSHU
Pacific Ocean
0
100
200 km
Life expectancy in Japan and the UK (years)
80
60
40
20
0
79
76
Japan
UK

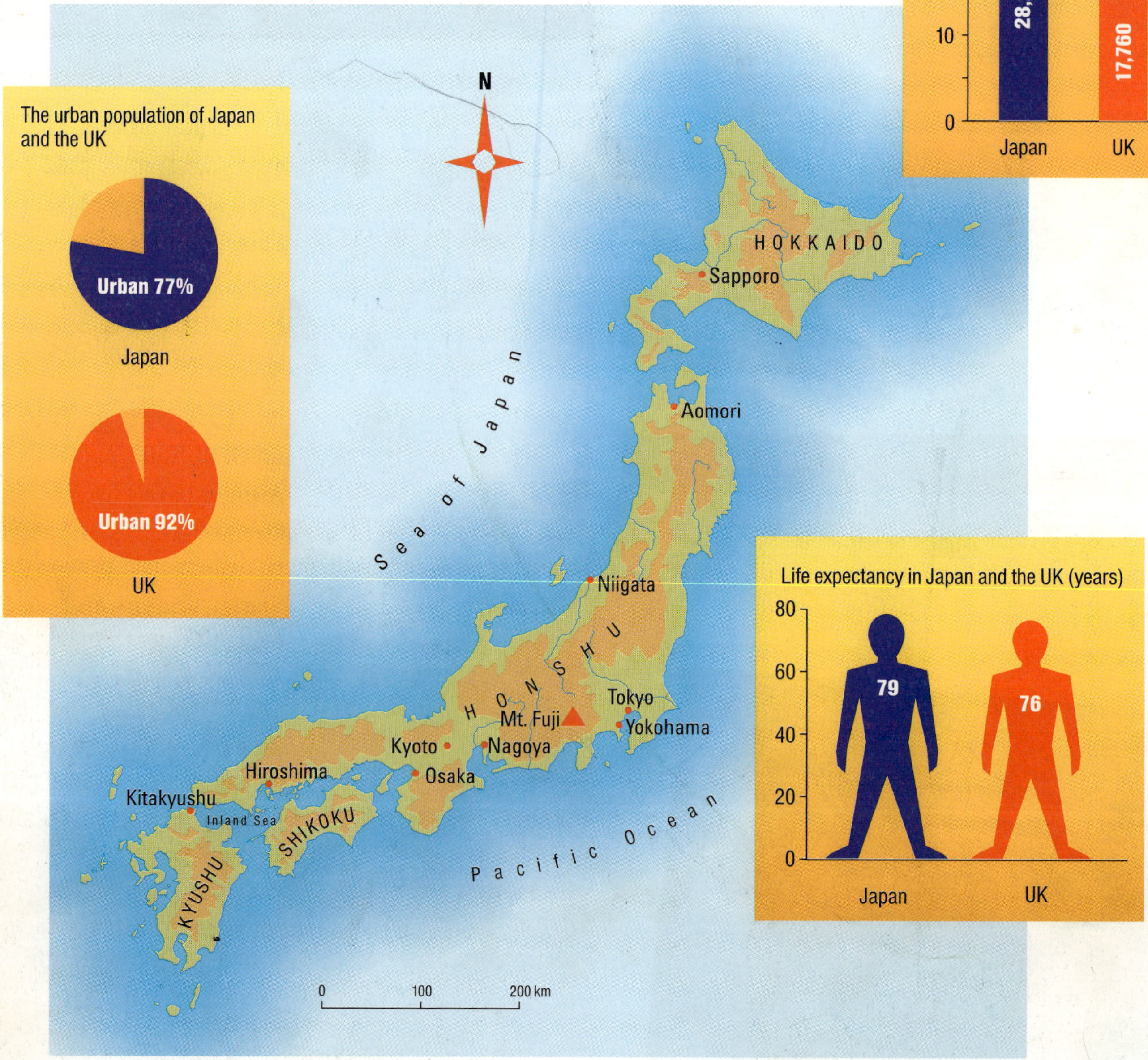

Activity 1

Here are the names of some major Japanese cities, the letters of which have been jumbled up. You will need Source 1 and an atlas to help you.

a) Unscramble each city.

b) Write out the name of the island and where it is.

c) Write a simple description of this location.

The first one has been done for you:

Koyto = **Tokyo** which is on **Honshu Island** and **faces the Pacific Ocean**.

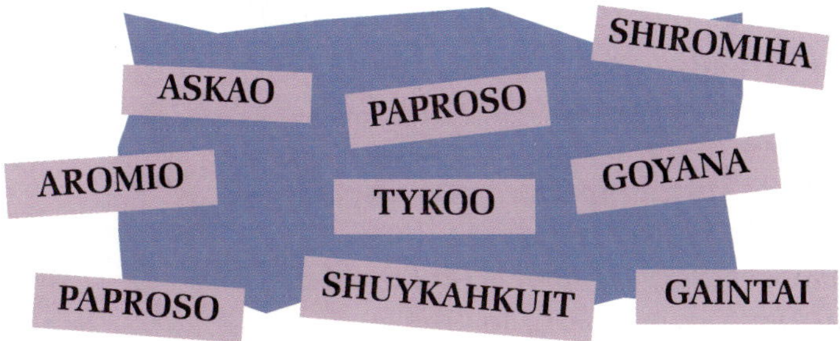

Source 2

Japan and the UK compared

	Japan	UK
Population in millions	125	58.4
Area in km^2	376,508	241,595
Density of people per km^2	33	241
% population growth	0.3	0.2
Literacy %	99	99

Activity 2

Use the data in Sources 1 and 2 to answer the following questions:

a) How much more does the average Japanese worker earn compared to someone in the UK?

b) In which country do most people live in cities?

c) Estimate how many times larger Japan's population is than the UK's.

d) Which country has the highest population density? Can you give reasons for this? The data on area will help you.

e) Write a few sentences comparing Japan with the UK.

Source 3

Mount Fuji is the highest peak in Japan. In Japan you are never far from either the sea or the mountains, but the natural environment can be a threat. Japanese people sometimes face earthquakes, volcanoes, tsunamis and typhoons.

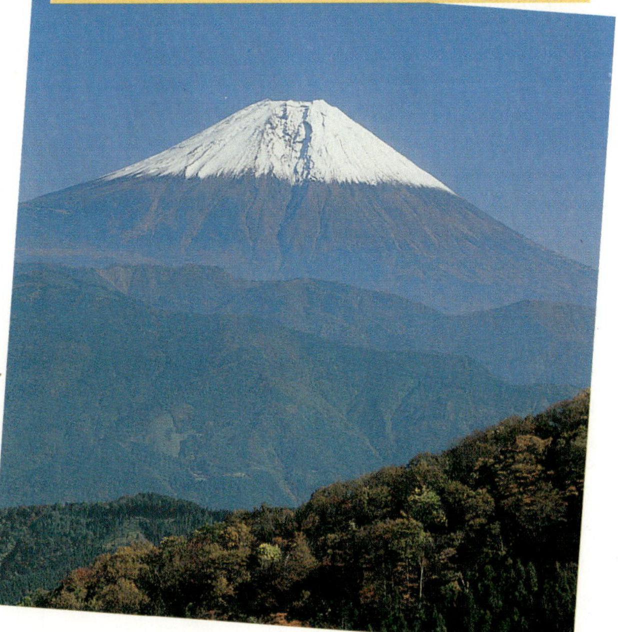

Source 4

Tokyo is a city that never sleeps. It is also extremely crowded, as this photo shows, and the buildings are closely packed together. Most city families have very small apartments. Houses with gardens are almost impossible to find.

Landscapes and hazards

Over three quarters of Japan is covered by mountains. Many rivers start in the mountains, flowing quickly on their short journeys to the sea. Flat, coastal lowland surrounds the mountains. The islands which make up the country stretch almost 3000 km from Hokkaido in the north to Okinawa in the south, over 25 degrees of latitude. Even Honshu, the largest island, is rarely wider than 300 kms.

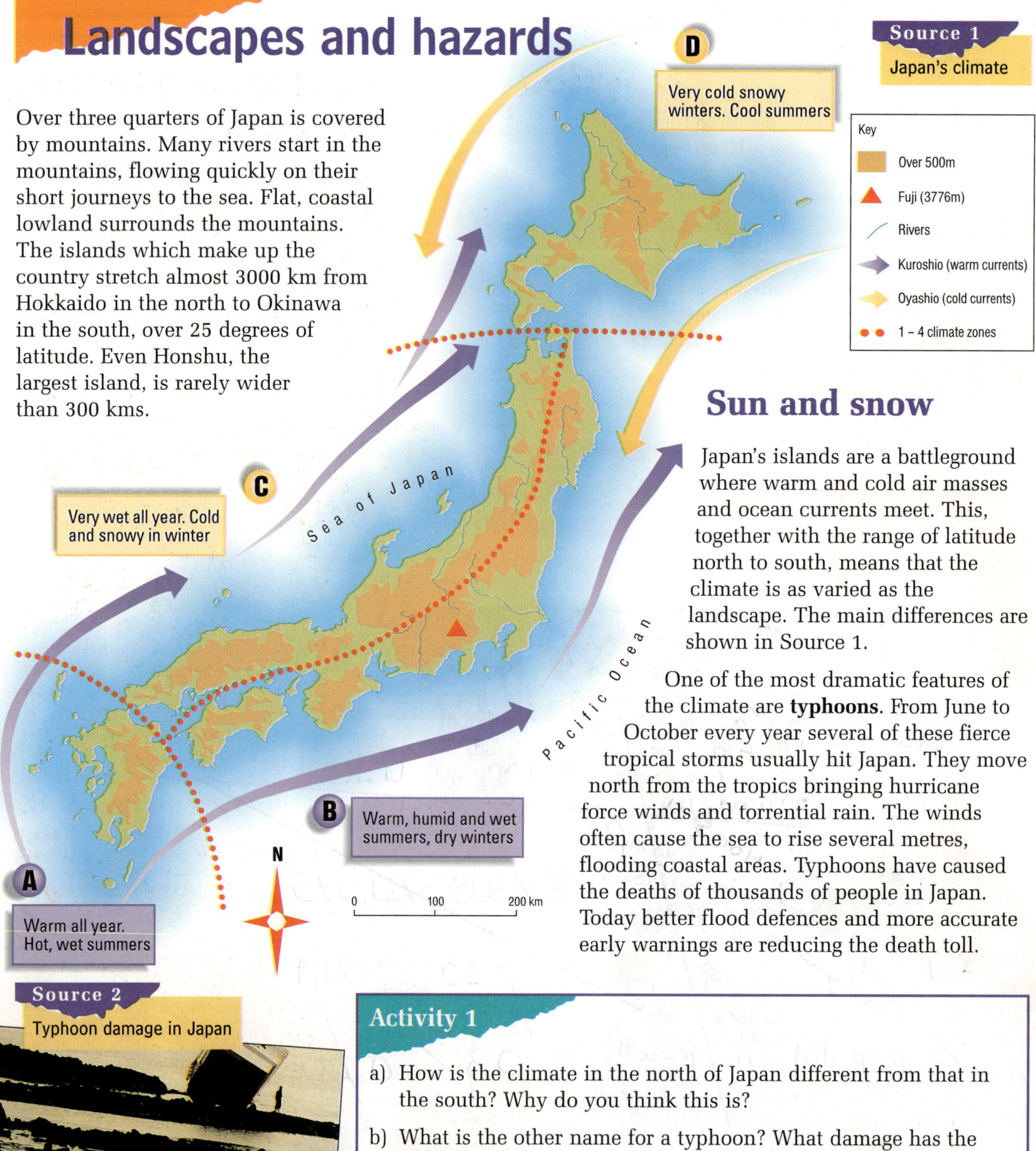

Sun and snow

Japan's islands are a battleground where warm and cold air masses and ocean currents meet. This, together with the range of latitude north to south, means that the climate is as varied as the landscape. The main differences are shown in Source 1.

One of the most dramatic features of the climate are **typhoons**. From June to October every year several of these fierce tropical storms usually hit Japan. They move north from the tropics bringing hurricane force winds and torrential rain. The winds often cause the sea to rise several metres, flooding coastal areas. Typhoons have caused the deaths of thousands of people in Japan. Today better flood defences and more accurate early warnings are reducing the death toll.

Source 2
Typhoon damage in Japan

Activity 1

a) How is the climate in the north of Japan different from that in the south? Why do you think this is?

b) What is the other name for a typhoon? What damage has the typhoon caused in Source 2. Suggest other sorts of danage which typhoons can cause.

c) Imagine you are a tourist staying in a hotel on the coast in Hokkaido. You hear a typhoon warning on the radio. As the typhoon approaches you make a telephone call home to describe what is happening. Write down your conversation.

TSUNAMI HITS HOKKAIDO. OVER 150 DEAD

Mount Unzen erupts. 41 killed

HUGE QUAKE DESTROYS TOKYO 100,000 DIE

Source 3

Earthquake damage

On the edge

Japan lies at the meeting point of several of the world's major **tectonic plates**. The movement and meeting of these giant plates causes earthquakes and volcanic activity. Japan has over seventy active volcanoes, including Mount Fuji (3774m), which overlooks Tokyo. Earthquakes are a more constant threat, with over 7000 each year, although many of these are quite small.

Source 4

Major natural disasters this century

Date	Event	Details
1914	Sakurajima, Kyushu.	Ash fell for over a year. Villages and farmland buried.
1923	Kanto Earthquake, Tokyo, 7.9 (Richter Scale).	Half a million houses destroyed. Landslides, fire.Over 100,000 dead.
1933	Tsunami on Sanriku coast.	Over 4,000 dead.
1948	Fukai earthquake, 7.1 (Richter Scale).	Nearly 4,000 dead.
1959	Ise Bay, Honshu (typhoon)	5,000 dead; 160,000 houses destroyed.
1983	Akita earthquake.	104 dead.
1988–1989	Mt.Tokachi, Hokkaido.	Over fifteen continuous major eruptions but no deaths.
1990 and 1993	Mt.Unzen, Kyushu.	Two major eruptions killed over 40 people; 10,000 evacuated.
1993	Tsunami hits Hokkaido (caused by 7.8 earthquake).	250 dead or missing. Buildings and ships destroyed. Widespread flooding.
1995	Earthquake at Kobe, 7.2 (Richter scale).	5,000 dead; and up to 100,000 homeless.

If an earthquake begins under the sea a **tsunami** may form. The sea rises quickly and makes a huge tidal wave. When it hits the land it can cause immense damage. On Hokkaido in 1993, a 30m high **tsunami** killed over 100 people.

Activity 2

On an outline map of Japan mark the location of each of the natural disasters in Source 4. Devise a symbol for each hazard (earthquake, typhoon, etc.,) and include the symbols in a key. Remember to give your map a title.

People patterns

Japan may not be one of the largest countries in the world, but there are only six countries which are more densely populated. Yet the population is not spread very evenly: 77 per cent of the people live on just 16 per cent of the land. As Source 2 shows, today's population of 124 million has doubled since the 1920s.

Source 1

A busy Tokyo street

Population structure

Japan's life expectancy of 79 years is the highest in the world. People today are living longer, and fewer babies are being born. Japan has a very low population growth rate. By the year 2015 Japan's total population is actually expected to start to fall.

The **population structure** is also changing. The number of old people (over 65 years) is expected to double by the year 2020. Looking after such large numbers of elderly people can put a lot of pressure on a country's resources.

Source 2

Population growth (millions)

Year	Population
1900	44
1910	50
1920	56
1930	64
1940	72
1950	83
1960	93
1970	104
1980	117
1990	124
* 2000	127
* 2010	129
* 2020	127

* (estimated)

Source 3

Population structures for 1950 and 1990 in Japan

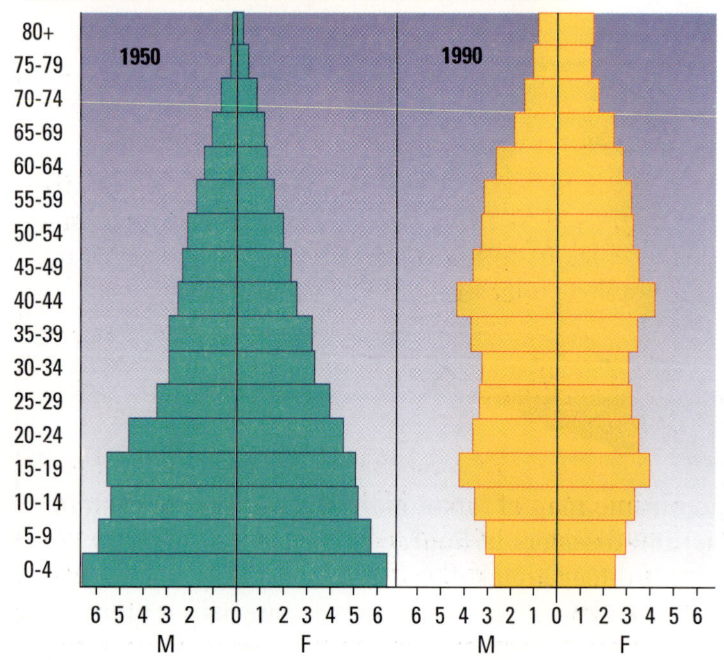

Activity 1

a) Use the figures in Source 2 to draw a line graph showing the actual and projected growth of Japan's population. Why do you think population growth is slowing down?

b) Look at the population structure graphs (Source 3).Describe the differences you can see in structure between 1950 and 1990.

Source 4

Large numbers of elderly people remain in more rural areas.

Source 5

A government official says ...

... THERE IS A LIMIT TO HOW MUCH MONEY CAN BE SPENT. CHOICES WILL HAVE TO BE MADE.
THERE WILL BE TWICE AS MANY ELDERLY PEOPLE IN JAPAN IN 20 YEARS TIME.

Moving to the cities

In the future Japan will have to cope with an increasingly old population. At the same time more and more people, especially the young, are moving to the cities to live and find work. This movement from rural to urban areas is called **urban drift** and is a problem in many countries.

Many people have moved to the urban area stretching from Tokyo to Kitakyushu. Places away from here are left with fewer people and many of those who remain are old. These places are often important for farming. As younger people move away it is becoming quite difficult for small, family-run farms to carry on.

Densely populated: a lot of people living in an area; crowded.

Growth rate: the speed at which the population is changing. Worked out by subtracting the death rate from the birth rate.

Population structure: the number of people of different ages and sexes in a country.

Urban drift: movement of people from the countryside (rural areas) to towns and cities (urban areas), often in search of work.

Activity 2

You have recently moved away from your family in a small farming village in the north of Japan to work in Tokyo. Write a letter home describing your experiences – good and bad.

Activity 3

Read carefully what the Government official is saying in Source 5. Make a list of some of the things Japan would have to spend more money on to look after the increased numbers of elderly people.

Crowded coast

Half of Japan's people live in the coastal lowlands, which stretch from Kyushu to Tokyo (see Source 1). This area is often called the Pacific Coastal Belt. When cities like Kyoto, Osaka and Kobe merge together they are called **conurbations**. If conurbations then join together, a **megalopolis** is created. The vast, unbroken urban sprawl from Kobe to Tokyo is known as the Tokaido Megalopolis.

Source 1
Japan's major cities

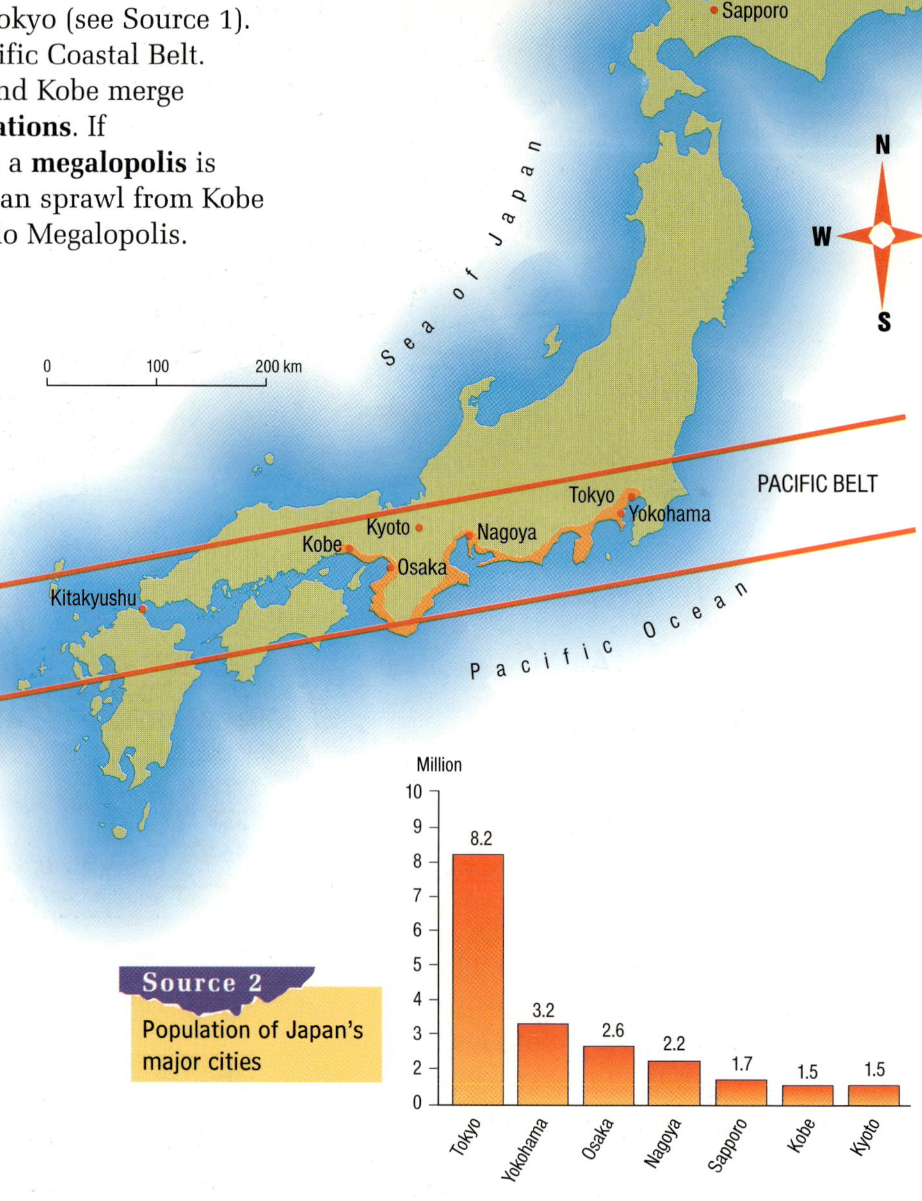

Source 2
Population of Japan's major cities

Source 3
The Tokaido Megalopolis

Activity 1

a) List as many words as you can to describe the urban landscape in Source 3.

b) Draw a table to show the good and the bad things about living in the megalopolis.

c) Explain why you would like (or not like) to live here.

Travelling in Tokyo

Dominating the area is Japan's capital city, Tokyo. Over 8 million people live here, making Tokyo the fourth largest city in the world. During the day the number of people in the city rises to 12 million as **commuters** who are unable to afford homes in the city travel to work. Journey times of over two hours are common. Travel by road can be even slower, despite new expressways.

Pressure on the land

Overcrowding can lead to other problems. In the 1960s smog became a major hazard in Japan as traffic and factories sent a continuous stream of gas and fumes into the atmosphere. Traffic police had to wear masks, and you could rarely see Mount Fuji. Strict new laws have helped to reduce pollution, particularly in Tokyo today.

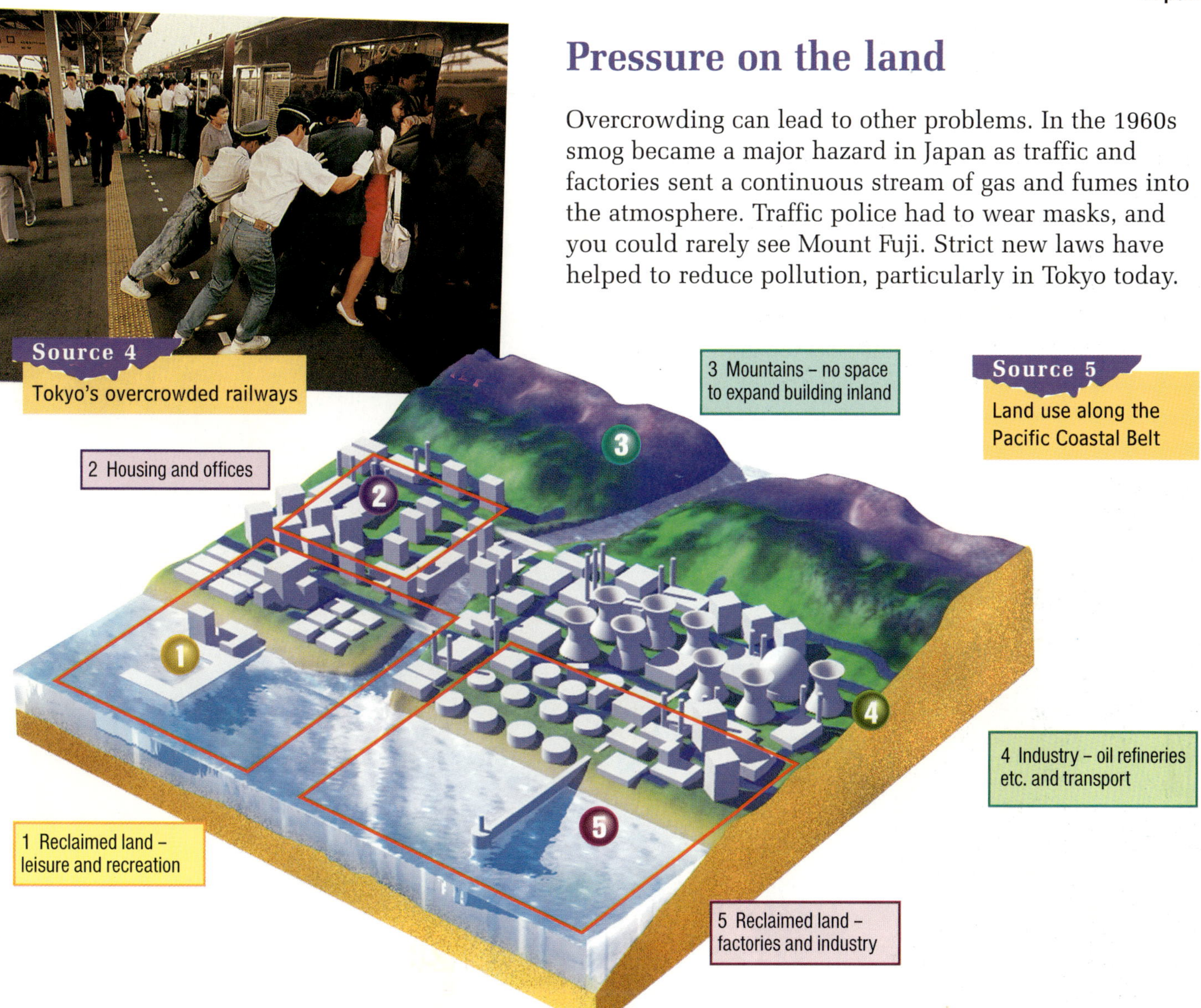

Source 4 Tokyo's overcrowded railways

Source 5 Land use along the Pacific Coastal Belt

Not only do vast numbers of people live on the Pacific Coastal Belt, but it is also home to most of Japan's industry. Older heavy industries like iron and steel and shipbuilding compete for land with newer car plants and high-tech industries. The pressure on the land is so great that new land is constantly **reclaimed** from the sea, for example in Tokyo Bay and Osaka Bay. In September 1994 the new Kansai International Airport (KIA) opened on land created in Osaka Bay.

Conurbation: large urban area formed when two or more cities merge together.

Expressway: Japanese motorway.

Megalopolis: when two or more conurbations join together.

Reclaimed land : new land created from the sea.

Activity 2

Using Source 5, describe some of the problems of living and working along the Pacific Coast of Japan.

Activity 3

Using your answer to Activity 2, write a page from a diary about a typical day along the Pacific Coast, written by a commuter travelling to work or by someone living in an apartment block

Japan unlimited

There can be few homes in Britain without any goods marked 'Made in Japan', or made by a Japanese company. TVs, videos, cameras, hi-fis, computers ... the list of Japanese-made electrical goods seems endless. Sony, Matsushita (Panasonic), NEC, Sharp, Toshiba, JVC and Hitachi are just some of the Japanese companies which are now familiar names in the UK. Companies like Nissan, Toyota, and Yamaha sell their cars and motorbikes throughout the world.

Source 1

UK soccer shirts display Japanese logos

Source 2

Japanese electrical goods

Why are these Japanese companies so successful? Although Japan has developed heavy industries such as iron and steel, shipbuilding and chemicals, it is in the high technology or 'high-tech' and car industries that Japan has made a real impact on world trade.

Activity 1

Collect photos or adverts of goods made by Japanese companies from newspapers and magazines. Make a collage of them, showing as wide a range of products and companies as possible.

Technology take-off

Japan is the world leader in the production of electronic goods. The development of high-tech 'sunrise' industries continues. Japan has few natural resources and high-tech industries do not rely on vast amounts of raw materials. Instead, high levels of investment, skilled labour and automation have brought progress. Money invested in research and development (R&D) has led to many new products such as the Sony Walkman, lap-top computers and a range of miniature cameras and TVs.

Activity 2

Copy out these statements, saying whether they are true or false:

- There are many natural resources in Japan.
- Japan's old, heavy industries include iron and steel, shipbuilding and chemicals.
- Skilled labour and the use of robots have helped Japan's new industries to develop.
- High-tech industries need lots of raw materials.
- Heavy investment in Research and Development has led to many new inventions.

Activity 3

Why do you think the name 'sunrise' is given to industries which are growing?

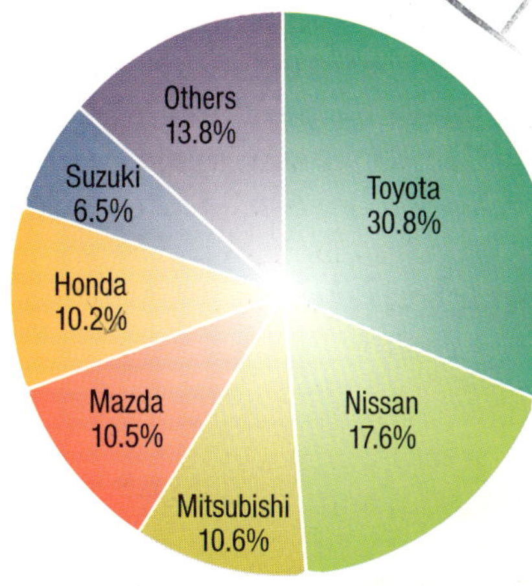

Source 3 Motor vehicle production in Japan in 1991

The motor industry

One in every ten Japanese workers is involved in the car industry. Source 3 shows Japan's top six car companies. By the beginning of the 1990s Toyota was selling more cars than the big American car makers. Efficiency and automation are the main reasons for this. Many Japanese car companies have now built factories in other countries. Toyota has two factories in the UK, one in Derbyshire and one in Deeside.

Source 4 An automated car production line

Source 5 Toyota fact file

Toyota Fact File ....

1918	Company founded
1937	Japan's first passenger car produced
1940's	Assembly-line mass production
1947	First small car
1960's	Toyota's production line systems improve e.g. 'just in time' component system
1970	Toyota factories built overseas
1991	Japan becomes world's leading producer of motor vehicles

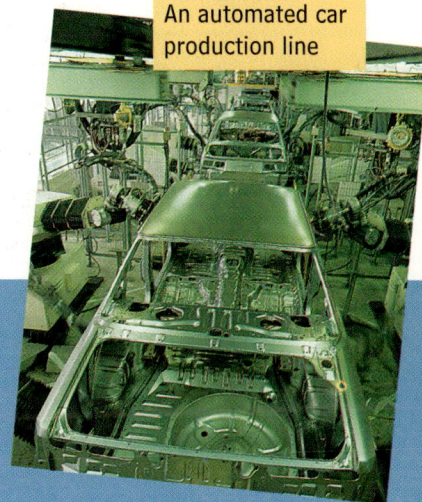

 Workforce — 72,000

 Car plants in Japan — 12 (around Toyota city, east of Nagoya) + 1 new plant on Kyushu

 Worldwide — Factories in 22 countries

 Other interests — Steel making, general engineering, rubber and housing

Activity 4

a) Choose a Japanese company other than Toyota to research. Put together a factfile like the one in Source 5.

b) Either design an advertisement to sell one of its newest products/models or produce a leaflet advertising the range of products produced.

Regional contrasts (1)

Like most countries, Japan is divided into a number of regions. There are eight main regions made up of forty-seven smaller units called **prefectures**. There are great variations between Japan's regions – differences in size, climate, population, wealth, facilities and employment.

Tokyo and Hokkaido compared

This unit looks at two areas, Hokkaido in Northern Japan, and Tokyo, part of the Kanto region of Honshu.

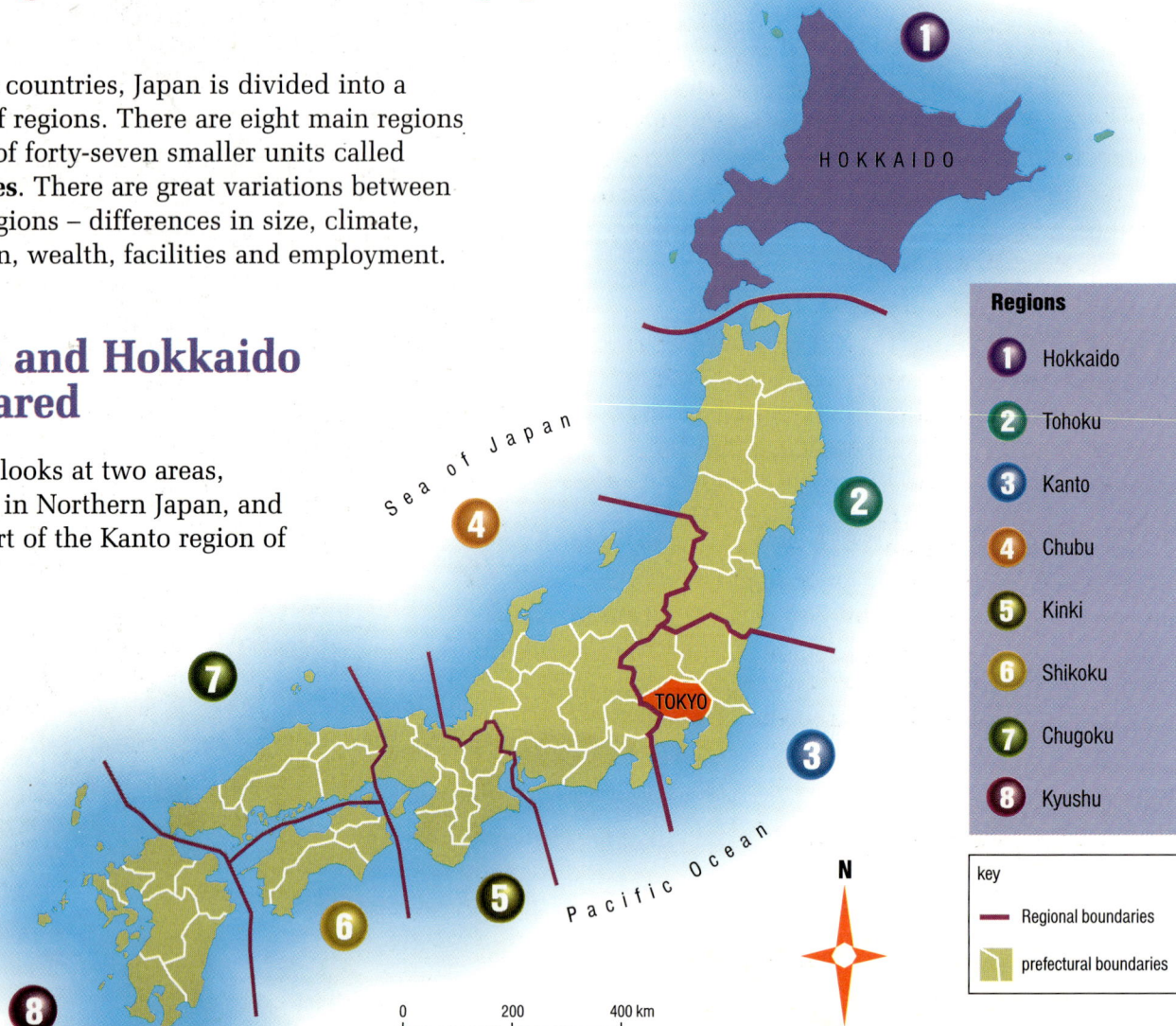

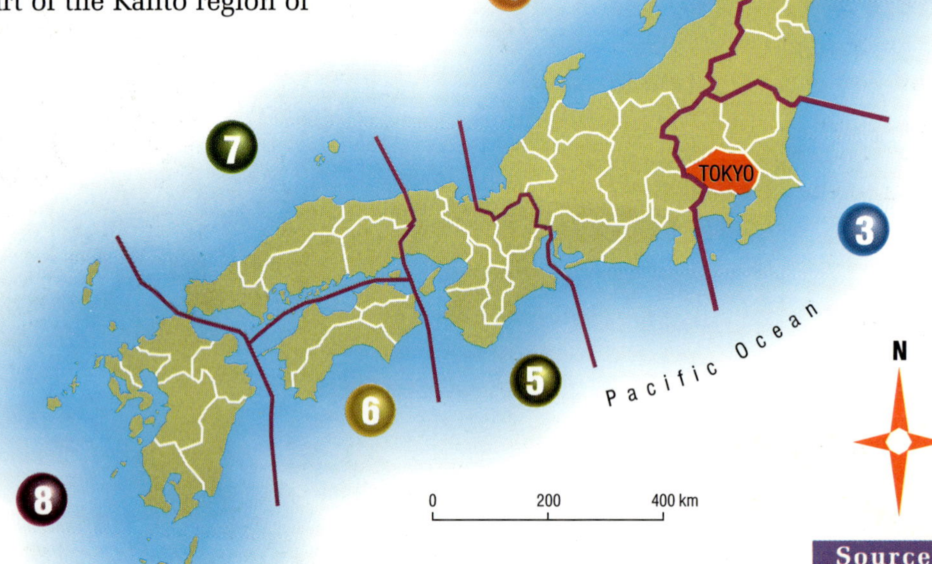

Source 1
Japan's regions and prefectures

Source 2
Fact file on Hokkaido and Tokyo

Hokkaido and Tokyo Fact File ....

Prefecture	Hokkaido	Tokyo
Size (km²)	78,413	2,183
% of Japan's land area	21.1	0.6
Population (millions)	5.6	11.8
% of Japan's population	4.5	9.6
Population density (people per km²)	72	5,430
Population over 65 years (%)	11.9	9.6

Activity 1

a) What can you tell about the two prefectures – Hokkaido and Tokyo – just by looking at the map (Source 1)? Think especially about their size and their position.

b) Now study the fact file (Source 2). Is there any other information which it might be useful to have?

Hokkaido

Hokkaido is Japan's most northerly region and the largest of the forty-seven prefectures. However, it is also the least densely populated, covering 21 per cent of the total land area, yet containing less than 1 per cent of the population. It is one of Japan's remotest areas, 750 kms from Tokyo. The opening of the Seikan rail tunnel in 1988 reduced the travel time between Hokkaido and Honshu.

High snow-capped mountains cover the centre of the island. They reach over 2000m. Winter sports like skiing are popular here – the 1972 Winter Olympics were based at Sapporo. In contrast, coastal areas are flat, and are important for farming. Hokkaido produces 10 per cent of the country's agricultural output. Dairy farming, and cultivation of cereals and root crops take place on farms which are much larger than elsewhere in Japan. Small amounts of oil and coal are found here. Mining and farming provide raw materials for local industry, although both coal mining and steel production have declined in recent years.

Source 3
Snow covered mountains in Hokkaido

Source 4
The climate in Sapporo, Hokkaido

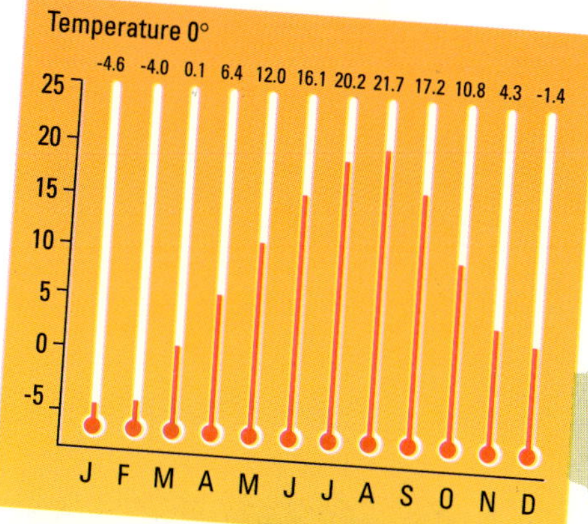

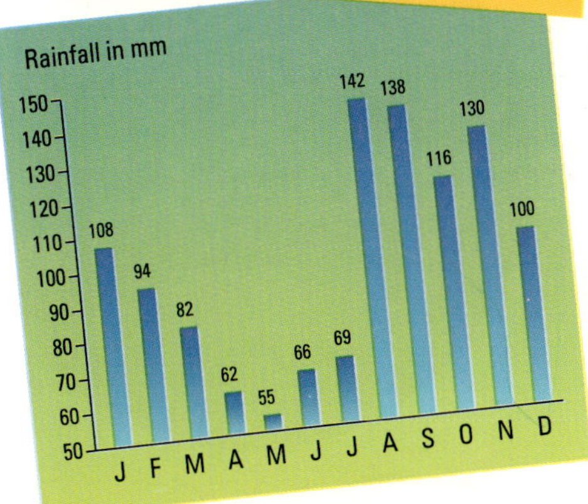

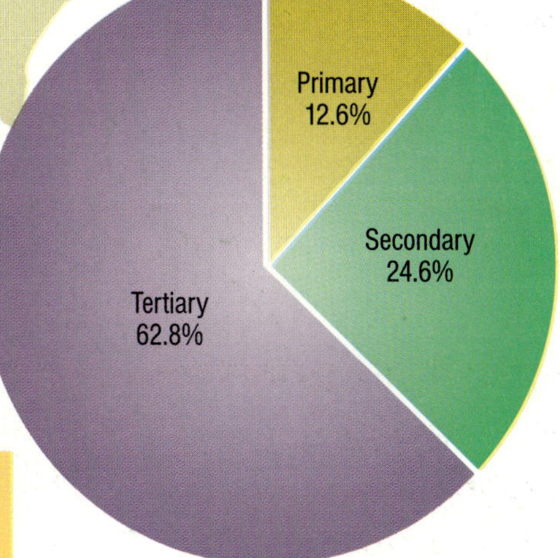

Source 5
The employment structure of Hokkaido

Regional contrasts (2)

Source 1
Tokyo roofscape

Source 2
Tokyo traffic

Tokyo

Tokyo is important not just as Japan's capital city, but as a world city (only New York, Los Angeles and Mexico City have more people). One in ten of Japan's population lives here. Tokyo is also the most densely populated prefecture in Japan. Its location on the wide Kanto plain on central Honshu's Pacific coast is one of the major reasons for its success. Flat land is in very short supply in this mountainous country.

Originally called Edo, the city was renamed Tokyo in 1868. It then became the political and financial centre of the country. In 1923, the Great Kanto Earthquake destroyed most of the area in and around Tokyo. Over 600,000 homes were lost, many as a result of the fires which broke out after the earthquake. Second World War bombing caused fresh damage. In the years after the war, Tokyo grew rapidly. Industry flourished along the coastal belt west of Tokyo and the population has almost doubled today from the 6.3 million total of 1950.

Many people work in the **tertiary** sector (see Source 4), often for small companies. Prices for land are high and many larger companies are beginning to move their factories and offices away from the city, although many still keep their head offices in the capital.

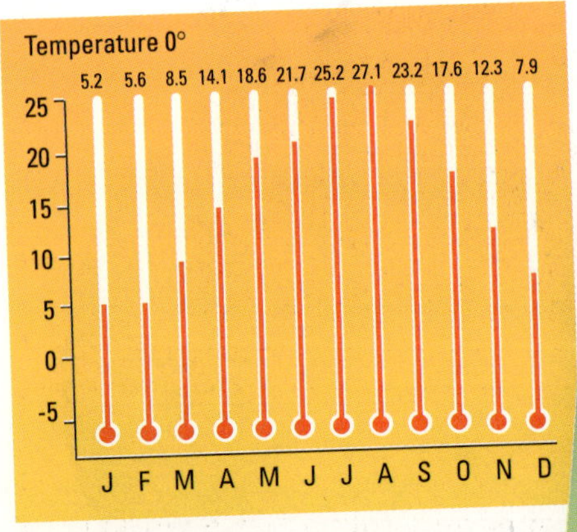

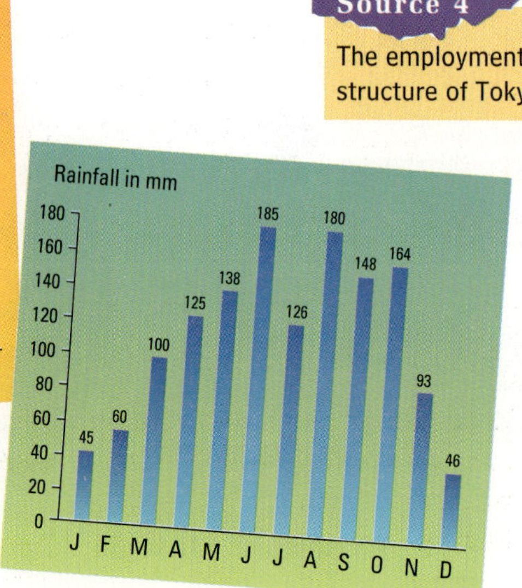

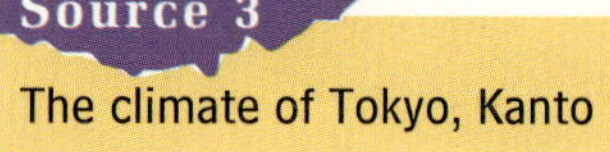
Source 3
The climate of Tokyo, Kanto

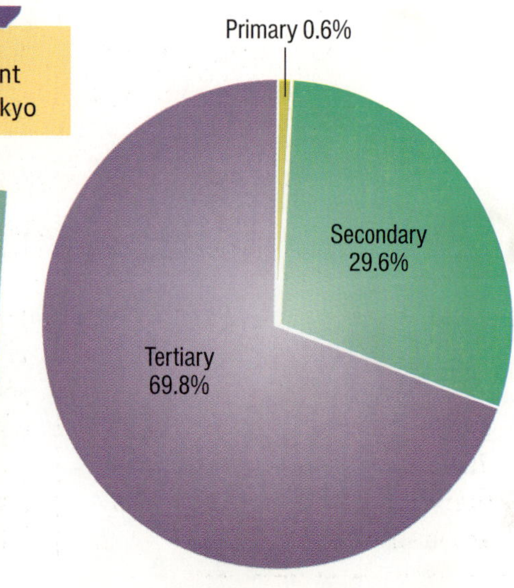

Source 4
The employment structure of Tokyo

Unlike many other cities in developed countries, Tokyo has no real centre. Instead there are many small 'sub-centres', often based around the main stations on Tokyo's vast railway system. Shops, shrines, offices, parks, factories and houses often seem mixed together. Tokyo's huge size has led to many problems, including overcrowding, strain on transport systems and pollution.

TOKYO IS SO CROWDED AND BUSY.
THE TRAFFIC IS TERRIBLE - AND THE NOISE AND FUMES.
THERE'S NO OPEN SPACE - JUST TALL BUILDINGS
PEOPLE ARE TOO BUSY TO MAKE FRIENDS.
EVERYTHING IS SO EXPENSIVE.

THE WEATHER IS VERY COLD - ESPECIALLY IN WINTER.
IT MUST BE VERY BORING AND QUIET.
THERE IS NOTHING TO DO - NOWHERE TO GO, ESPECIALLY FOR YOUNG PEOPLE
IT IS SUCH A LONG WAY FROM EVERYWHERE.

Source 5

A Hokkaido farmer talking about Tokyo and a Tokyo office worker talking about Hokkaido

Activity 1

Look at the list of statements below. Some are in the correct column – others are not. Copy out the table, putting each statement under the correct heading.

Tokyo v	Hokkaido
very densely populated	21 per cent of Japan's land area
larger % over 65 years	most important farming area in Japan
almost no primary industry	less than 6 million people
very cold winters	warm, wet summers
remote	accessible
built on flat land	mainly mountainous
political and financial centre	location of 1972 winter Olympics

Activity 2

Tokyo and Hokkaido are different in many ways. Are there any ways in which they are similar?

Activity 3

Read carefully what the Hokkaido farmer and Tokyo office worker are saying. They are being quite negative about each other's home region. Write down what they might say to one another in reply, talking about the GOOD things about their own region.

Trading nation

The Japanese have always been a nation of traders. Over 500 years ago, they sold fine steel goods like swords to other countries. Now it is TVs, computers and cars. As the type of product has changed, the value of Japan's exports has rocketed. Today Japan is responsible for 9 per cent of the world's exports and 6.5 per cent of the world's imports. Yet Japan has very few natural resources. Raw materials need to be imported so that Japanese factories can produce goods to sell at home and abroad. With limited land available for farming, food is another major import.

Source 1

Oil refineries in Japan

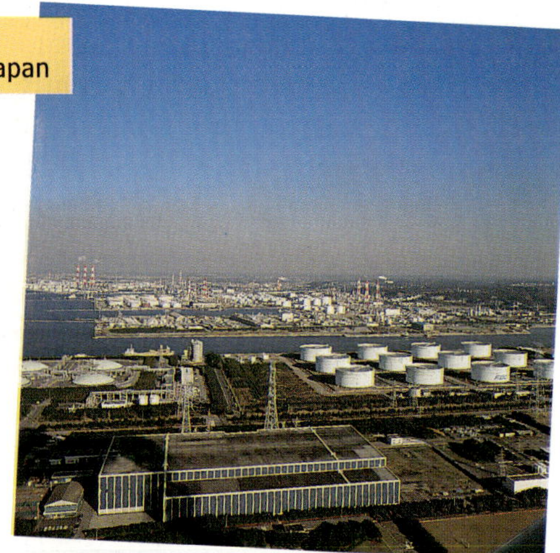

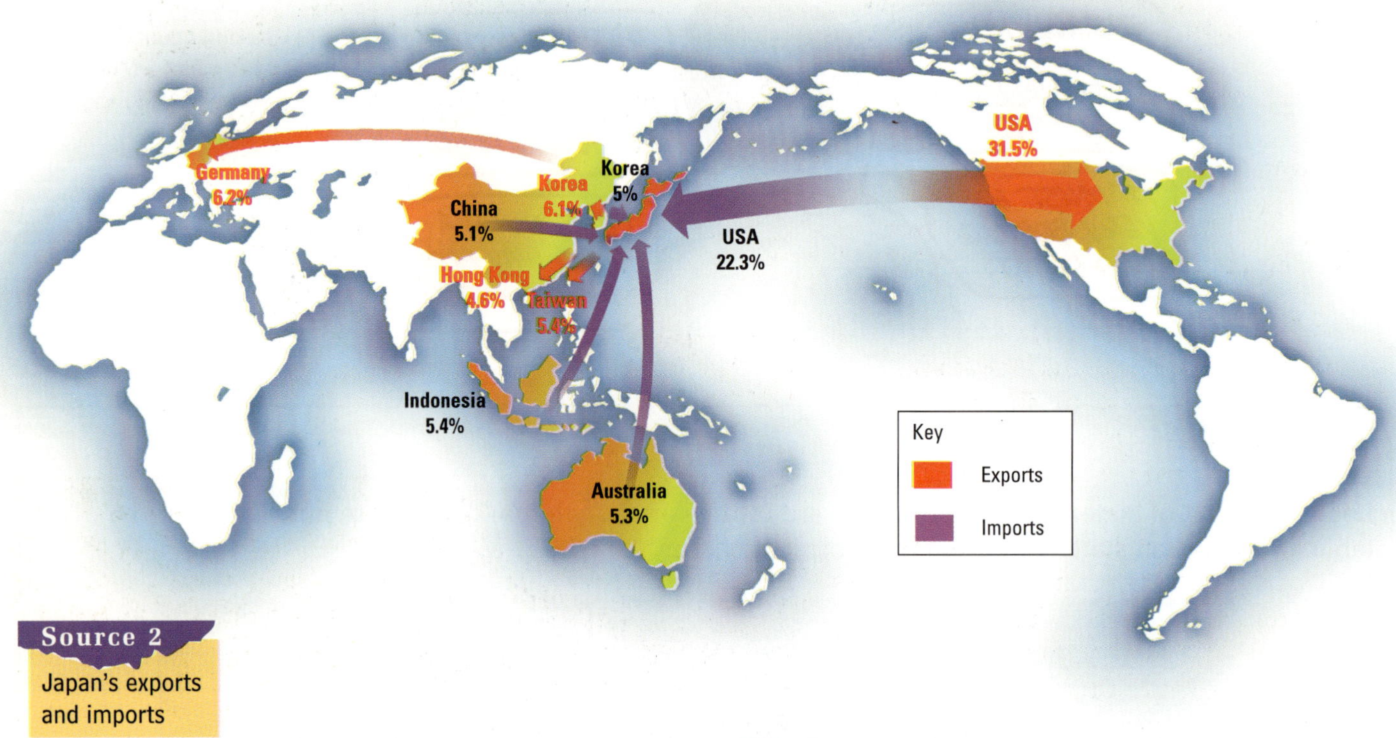

Source 2

Japan's exports and imports

Japan in Asia

Although the map (Source 2) shows that the USA is Japan's most important trading partner, imports and exports to and from nearby countries have increased in recent years. Today over 50 per cent of Japan's trade is with its Asian neighbours. Japan may dominate trade in this part of the world today, but China and Korea are growing in importance.

Activity 1

a) Look at Source 1. Japan has many oil refineries like these but almost no oil is found in Japan. The Japanese are worried that they need to import so much oil – why do you think this is?

b) Write a report from the Japanese Minister for Energy to the Japanese government. Try to explain why the country should reduce oil imports. Suggest how energy could be saved and what other energy sources could be used instead.

Source 3

A Japanese port

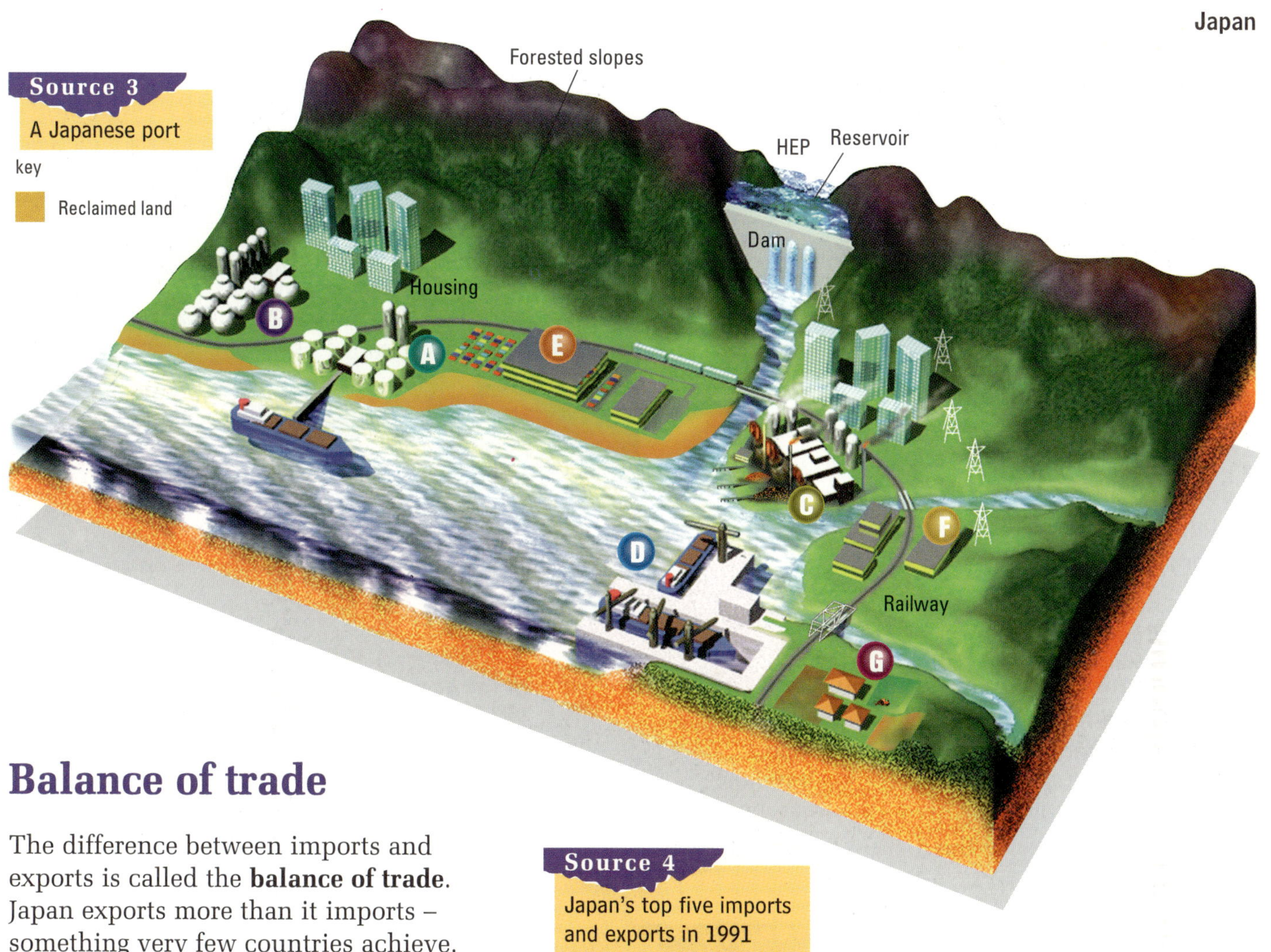

Balance of trade

The difference between imports and exports is called the **balance of trade**. Japan exports more than it imports – something very few countries achieve. This gives it a **trade surplus**. When imports are higher than exports, a trade deficit results. Japan's surplus is partly due to the government restricting some imports. Countries such as the USA are beginning to put pressure on Japan to lift restrictions. Japan banned imports of rice until recently, but limited amounts are now allowed in.

Source 4

Japan's top five imports and exports in 1991

Imports	Exports
Machinery & equipment	Cars
Food	Iron & steel products
Oil	Textiles
Chemicals	Ships
Metal ores	Electrical goods

Activity 2

Using Sources 3 and 4 answer the following:

a) What goods might the ship be carrying from abroad to A, B and C?

b) What is being produced at D, E and F for export?

c) Farming is taking place at G. Why do you think food is such a major import?

Balance of trade: the difference between the value of your imports and your exports. Can be negative or positive.

Export: to sell goods abroad.

Import: to buy in goods from another country.

Trade deficit: to buy more than you sell

Trade surplus: to sell more than you buy.

Japan abroad

Many of us own products made by Japanese companies, but they are not necessarily 'Made in Japan'. Since the 1970s, many Japanese companies have built factories abroad. This has been encouraged by the Japanese government.

There are many advantages in building factories abroad. Land and labour costs are often lower than in Japan. Foreign or local governments may offer financial incentives – low rents and grants. By building in other countries, import taxes may be avoided. Large new markets may be opened up for Japanese products.

Source 1

A Japanese company in the UK

Many of the companies with factories abroad are **multinational companies**. A multinational company is a large, world-wide organisation. Some handle more money every year than many countries! Japan has thirteen companies listed in the world's top fifty multinationals. Toyota, at fifth place, is the highest Japanese company on the list.

Source 2

Toyota abroad

Fact File . . . .

Workforce	100,000
No. of countries	22
No. of factories	34
Car production 1991	670,000

Source 3

Toyota round the world

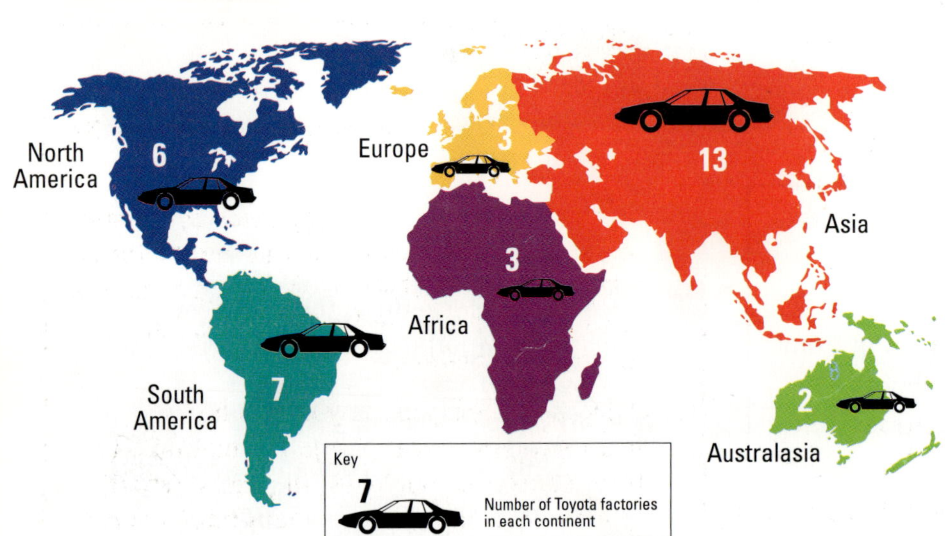

Activity 1

a) What advantages do Japanese companies gain by building factories abroad?

b) (i) List any items in your home or owned by your family which were made by a Japanese company.

(ii) Look carefully at each one to see where it was made. Make a list of the different countries you find. You could present this work as a table.

Japan UK

In the last few years, many famous Japanese companies have built factories in the UK. There are nearly 150 in total, employing over 25,000 people. They produce goods such as cars, tyres, and electrical items. South Wales, the Midlands and the North East are the most popular locations in the UK for Japanese companies. Sony, Mitsubishi, Nissan and Toyota are all located here.

Source 4

European workers in a Japanese factory

Financial incentives: money or grants offered to companies to encourage them to choose a particular location for its factories.

Market: the people or companies who buy the goods you make

Multinational (transnational) company: a company that operates in many countries.

Case Study Toyota

Toyota has built two large factories in the UK. There is an engine plant on Deeside in North Wales and a car factory in Burnaston, Derbyshire. The target for the factories is 200,000 cars and 200,000 engines a year. These factories provide work for over 3,000 people, many of whom were already skilled workers. The company sometimes sends its workers for training to its factories in Japan. Toyota chose to locate these two factories in the UK because :

- it is a good market for its cars;
- it has easy access to the rest of Europe;
- it was encouraged by the UK Government and local authorities.

By 1995 Toyota plans that 80 per cent of the parts used to make its cars in the UK will be from the UK or Europe, providing more work in the UK.

Activity 2

a) Why has Toyota chosen the UK for two of its car factories?

b) Find out if there are any Japanese companies in your area. You could look at the Business telephone directories under company names, or in Yellow Pages under Car dealers or Electrical suppliers.

c) A Japanese company is going to build a factory in your area. Is this a good or a bad thing? Discuss your ideas in pairs or small groups. Make a list of the main points and present them to the class.

Tokyo v Osaka: battle of the giants

For many years Tokyo, at the eastern end of the vast Tokaido megalopolis, has been the centre for Japanese business. It has been the automatic choice of Japanese companies as the place to locate their head offices. However, in September 1994 the new Kansai International airport opened on reclaimed land in Osaka Bay, 600 km west of Tokyo. The airport is one of many major projects planned for the Kansai region around Osaka.

Here we look at the advantages and disadvantages of locating a company in Tokyo or in Rinku Town, a new town being built near the new airport in Osaka Bay.

Source 1

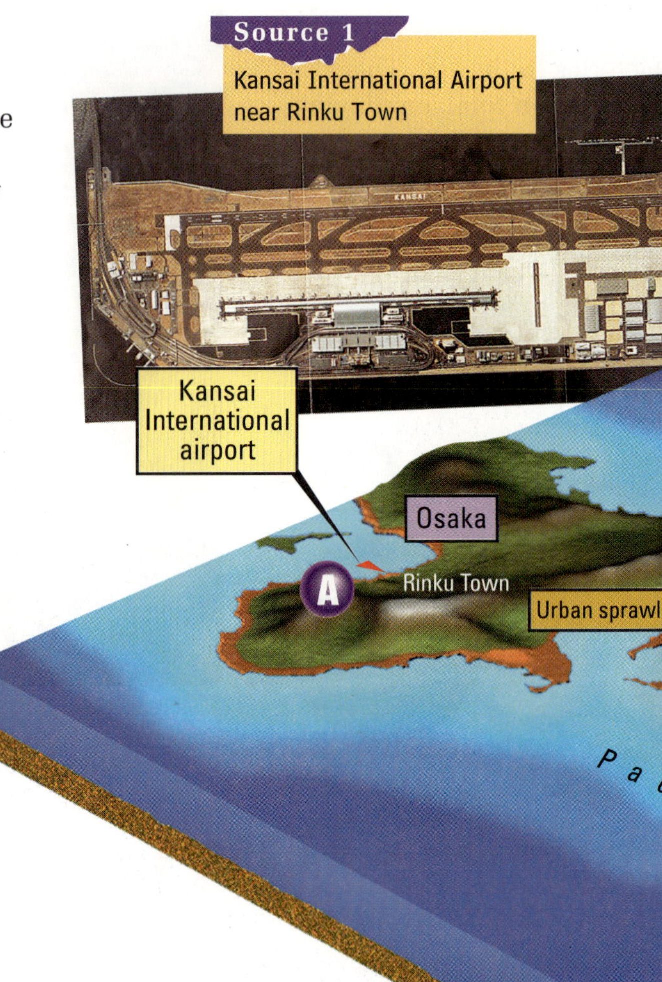

Kansai International Airport near Rinku Town

Rinku (new) Town, Osaka

- Skilled workforce needed
- More space
- Local hostility
- Good transport links to the rest of Japan
- New state-of the art facilities
- New development may have teething problems
- Cheaper than Tokyo
- A 45-minute journey to Osaka
- A long way from Tokyo
- Less 'red tape' (bureaucracy) for businesses
- The new 'Pacific City' of the future
- Next to the new Kansai International airport
- Grants from Osaka Prefectural Government

Activity

Either:

You are the chairman of a Japanese company. The company is small but hopes to expand quickly. It needs new offices and a factory area to make components for the computer industry. Choose a location for your company, either in Tokyo or Rinku Town. Write a report to present to the company explaining the reasons for your choice. The report should look at the good and bad points of both areas.

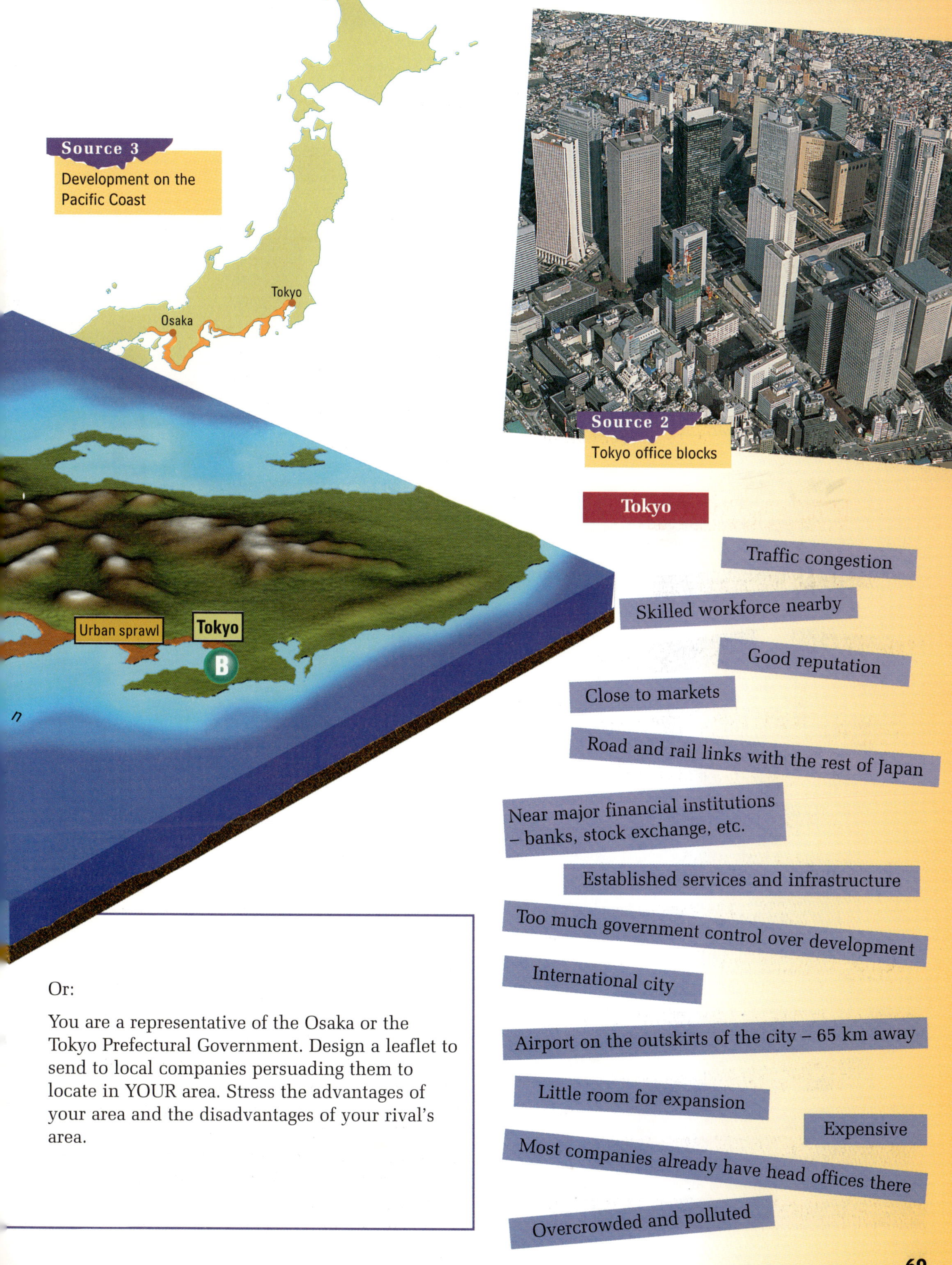

Or:

You are a representative of the Osaka or the Tokyo Prefectural Government. Design a leaflet to send to local companies persuading them to locate in YOUR area. Stress the advantages of your area and the disadvantages of your rival's area.

Kenya

Kenya is in East Africa, on the Equator. It is well-known throughout the world as home of the safari, and is increasingly popular with tourists. What attracts people to Kenya? Apart from wildlife, there is a spectacular natural environment which includes the Great Rift Valley and the peaks of Mount Kenya. There are also many tribal groups. Amongst the most famous are the Maasai to the south and the Kikuyu who live close to Mount Kenya. The two major cities are Nairobi, the capital, and Mombasa on the coast. This unit investigates some of the different faces of this diverse country.

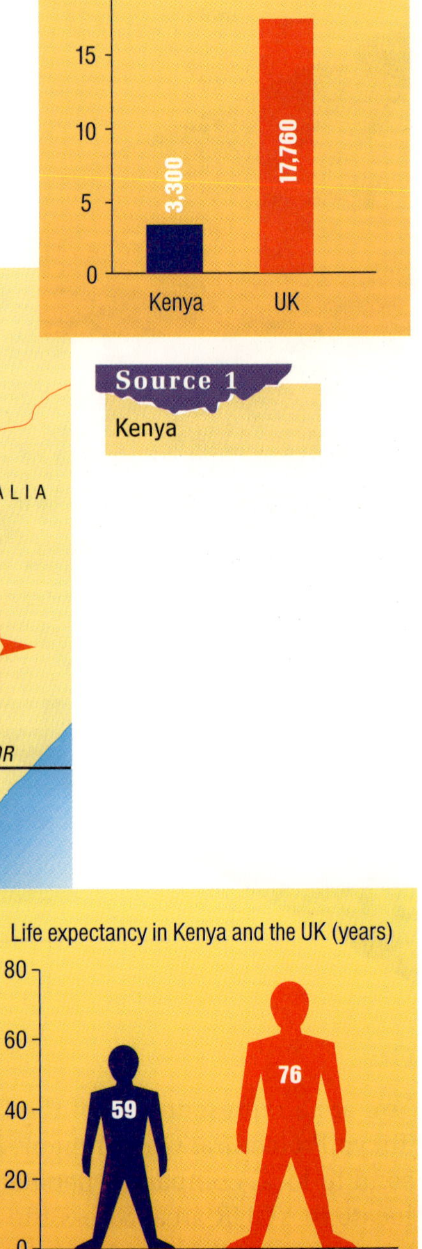

ETHIOPIA
SUDAN
0 100 200 km
Key
Highland
Capital city
City
Lake Turkana
SOMALIA
N
KENYA
UGANDA
THE EQUATOR
Mt. Kenya 5199m
River Tana
Lake Victoria
Nairobi
TANZANIA
Mombasa

The urban population of Kenya and the UK

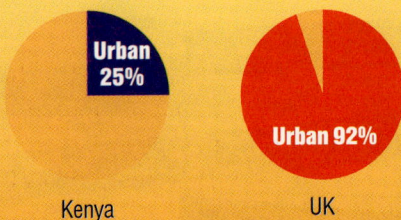

Urban 25%
Urban 92%
Kenya
UK

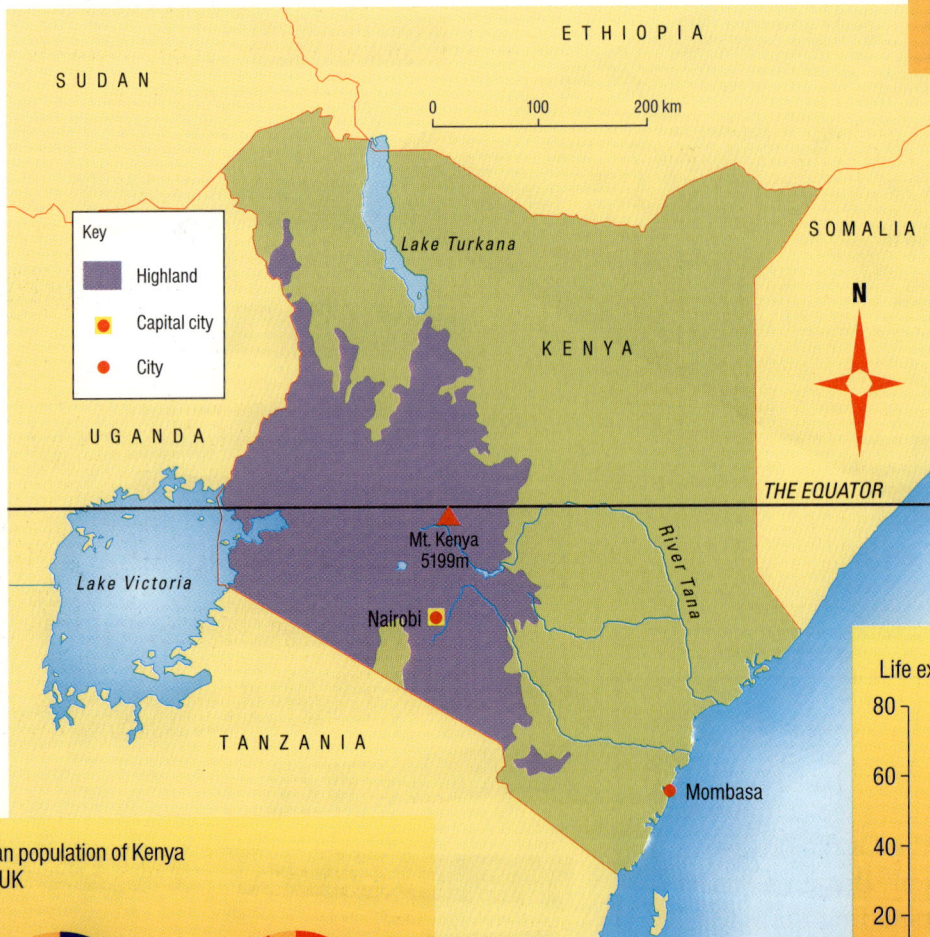

Activity 1

Study the map of Kenya (Source 1), then copy and complete the following paragraph:

Kenya has two main cities.________________ is the capital and ___________________ on the coast is a popular tourist destination. Kenya shares a border with: ________________, _____________, Ethiopia, ________________ and ______________. At 5200m _________________ is the highest mountain in the country. Lake _____________ lies to the south west of Kenya.

Activity 2

Below you will find eight sentences about Kenya. Some are incorrect. Using the data box (Source 2) and the information in Source 1, spot the mistakes.

- Kenya is half the size of the UK.
- The UK is almost six times richer than Kenya.
- Most people in Kenya live in the countryside.
- The UK's population is growing faster than Kenya's.
- Kenya is smaller than the UK.
- People live longer in Kenya.
- The UK is more crowded than Kenya.
- 99 per cent of the people in Kenya can read.

Now write out all the sentences correctly.

Source 2

Kenya and the UK compared

	Kenya	UK
Population in millions	27	58.4
Area in km^2	569,696	241,595
Density of people per km^2	47.3	241
% population growth	3.3	0.2
Literacy (%)	70,5	99

Source 4

Nairobi is a lively city. This photograph shows the modern side of the city.

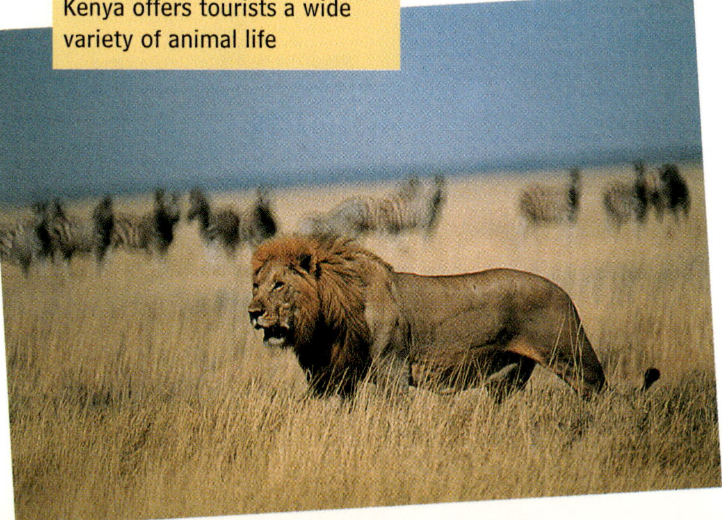

Source 3

Simba means 'lion' in Swahili. Kenya offers tourists a wide variety of animal life

Activity 3

Imagine you are on holiday in Kenya. Use the information and photographs on this page to help you write a postcard home which describes the country. You could also do some research in holiday brochures to help you.

Landscapes and climates

Kenya's landscapes are exciting and varied. Mount Kenya (5199 m) dominates the central highland. It was once an old volcano but today it is covered in snow and has its own **glacier**. Another major feature is the **Great Rift Valley**, see Source 1. It runs from north to south and is so large it can be seen from space.

The north and east of Kenya is much flatter than the centre. There is little rainfall, so much of the land turns to desert. Just offshore, in the warm waters of the Indian Ocean, is a beautiful coral **reef**.

Source 1

The Rift Valley

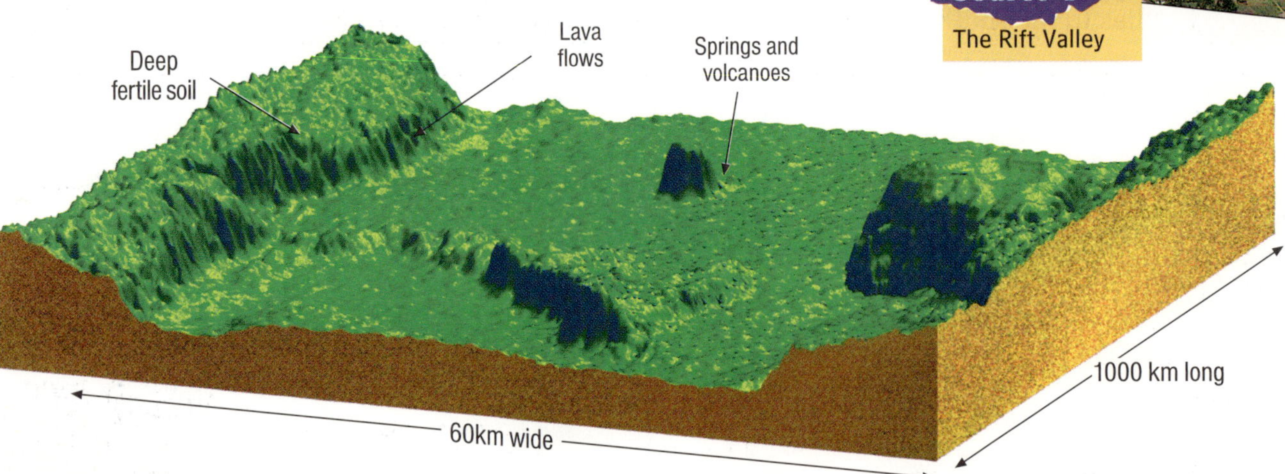

Activity 1

Look at the sketch of the Rift Valley (Source 1).

a) What will you find on the floor of the Valley?

b) Where do you think the lava came from?

c) Why can the Rift Valley be seen from space?

Activity 2

Imagine you are exploring Kenya. You have climbed Mount Kenya. Complete your diary with a description of what you can see. Use the information on this page and the map (Source 1) on page 70.

Begin the entry like this:

'I'm lucky because today the clouds have cleared and I can see …'

Climate

Kenya is on the equator. This means that average temperatures are high, and remain the same all year. Even here though, temperatures can vary. Why do you think Mount Kenya is covered in snow?

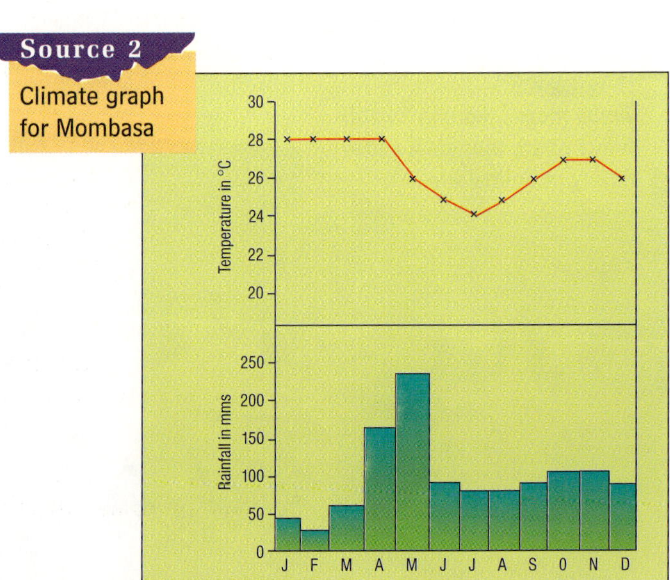

Source 2

Climate graph for Mombasa

What is the climate like?

'On a typical day in Nairobi, you wake up in the morning and the sky is bright and clear. But by the afternoon clouds will have built up and there will be a thunderstorm. And then in the evening it's dry again. Of course, not all of Kenya is like this. The highlands are wetter and cooler and the coast is much warmer.'

Source 3

Climate statistics for Nairobi (1820m above sea level)

	J	F	M	A	M	J	J	A	S	O	N	D
Temperature (°C)	18	19	19	19	18	17	16	16	17	18	18	18
Rainfall (mm)	37	54	132	196	136	41	19	25	23	49	100	64

Activity 3

a) Use the information in Source 3 to draw a graph for temperature and rainfall in Nairobi. Use the same style as we used in the climate graph in Source 2.

b) Write a few sentences comparing the climate graph for Mombasa with your graph for Nairobi.

Vegetation

Without water, few things can grow. Much of Kenya is very dry, but plants can adapt to these conditions.

Source 4

Vegetation in the savannah

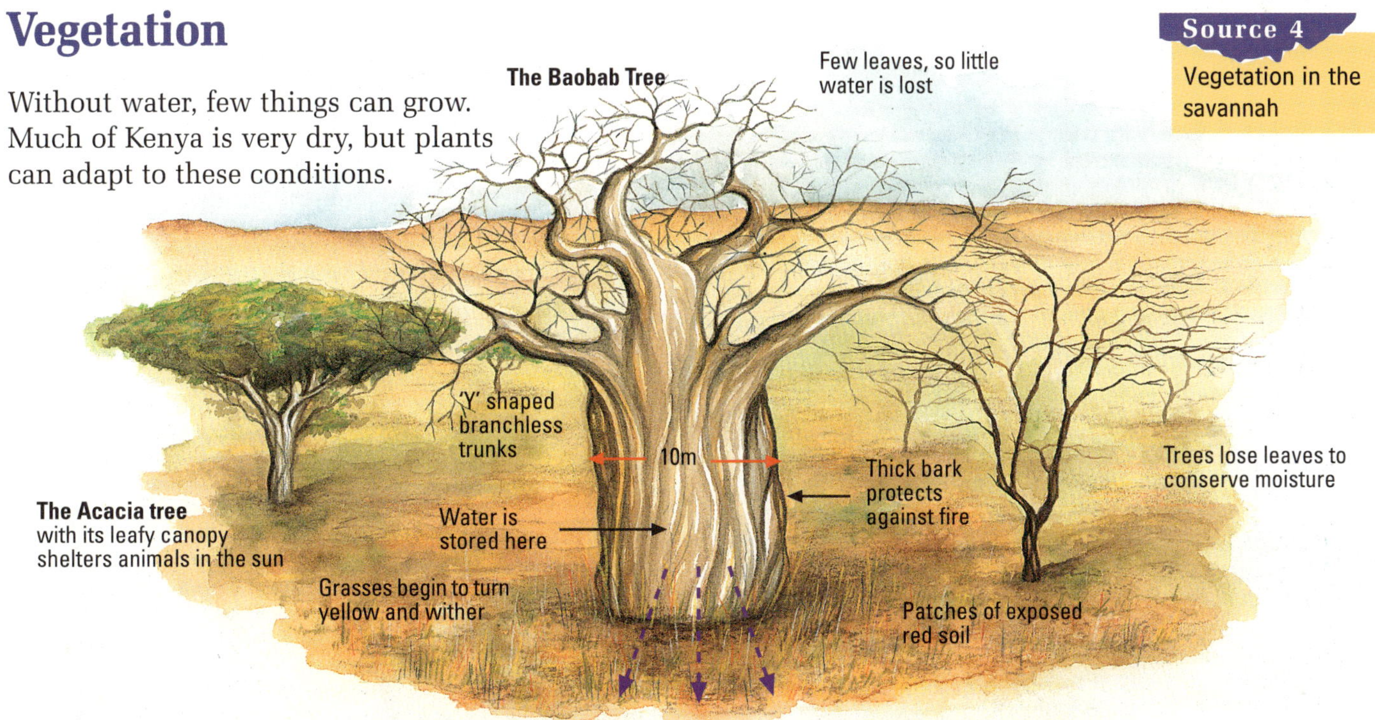

Activity 4

Look at Source 4 and the description of savannah plants:

a) Write down the phrases that tell you how these plants can survive with little water.

b) Why do you think the baobab is called the 'Bottle tree'?

West to East across Kenya

A day's journey inland from Kenya's Indian Ocean coastline takes you through two very different regions: the coastal area around Mombasa and the inland tea growing region of Kericho. The map (Source 1) shows where they are located.

Source 1

The regions located

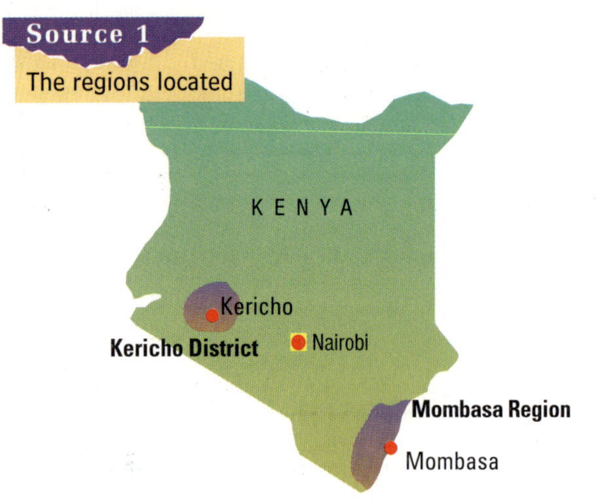

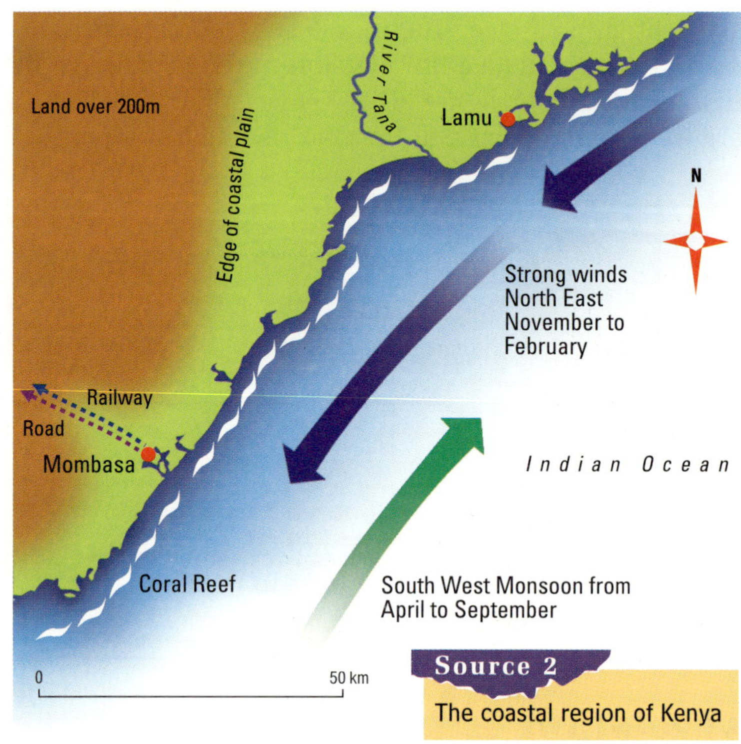

Source 2

The coastal region of Kenya

On the coast: Mombasa

Mombasa is the second largest city in Kenya (population 520 000). It became an important port because of the deep waters and the break in the coral reef. This has attracted factories and an oil refinery to the city.

Tourism is expanding here. Visitors are attracted by the long sandy beaches where they can enjoy swimming and diving. Marine parks at Watamu and Malindi help protect the coral reef.

Activity 1

Use the Sources and text to help you to fill the gaps.

a) The coastal district is on the _______ Ocean.

b) The lowlands are widest in the __________ and narrow near the Tanzanian border.

c) The marine parks at ____________ and ____________ help protect the __________ reef.

What is Mombasa like?

Mombasa's climate is hot and humid, and the vegetation is thick and green. Farmers here grow tropical fruits like mangoes, vegetables, cashew nuts, cotton and coconuts. These are sold in Mombasa and Nairobi, and some of this produce is sent to London. How many of these can you buy in your supermarket?

Source 3

Mombasa town and harbour

Up in the hills: Kericho

Kericho district lies to the west of the Rift Valley. It is about 2000 m above sea level. This makes the temperature cooler. Here there is more rainfall than on the coast. The whole area was once covered in forests, but most of these were cleared to grow tea. Kericho is the centre of tea production. Most tea used to be grown on large **plantations**. These are large farms containing their own factories, workers' housing, a shop, a hospital and schools. Brooke Bond owned plantations here, which helped to develop the town. Today, small farmers are responsible for growing most of Kenya's tea.

Follow the cartoon (Source 5) to see how tea is grown today:

Source 4

The Kericho region

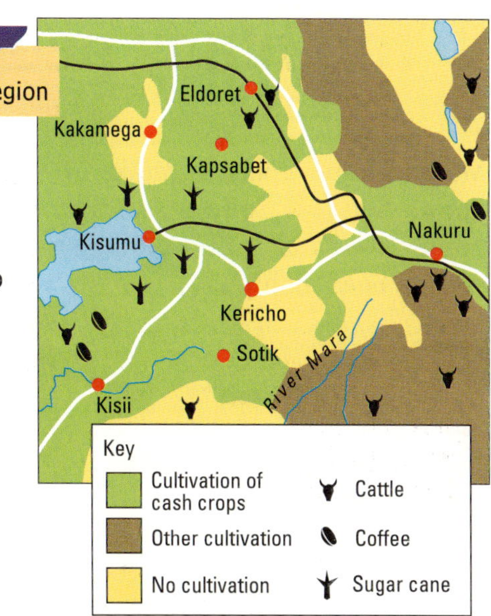

Source 5

Producing tea

Activity 2

a) Study the cartoon above (Source 5). Use it to describe the journey that a tea leaf makes before reaching your breakfast table

b) Look at the diagram below. How much tea is produced?

c) What has happened to Kenya's tea production since 1970?

38,000 tonnes

1970

Activity 3

Below are some phrases which describe either the Coastal region or the Kericho district. They are jumbled up. Copy and complete the table, putting the words in the correct column:

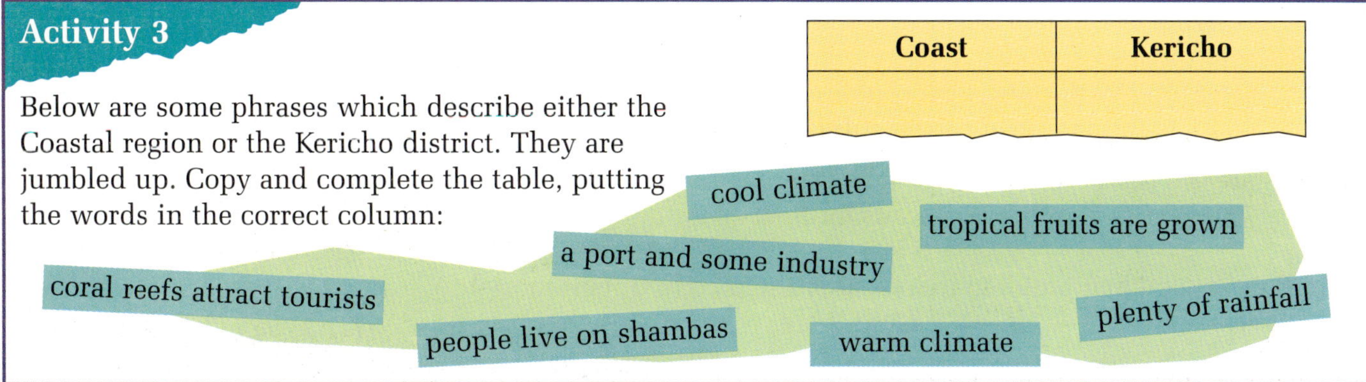

Coast	Kericho

Too many people?

Many different peoples make up Kenya's population (see Source 1). Today Kenya's population is 27 million, but it has not always been as high.

Source 1
Kenya's peoples

Arab

Maasai

Luo

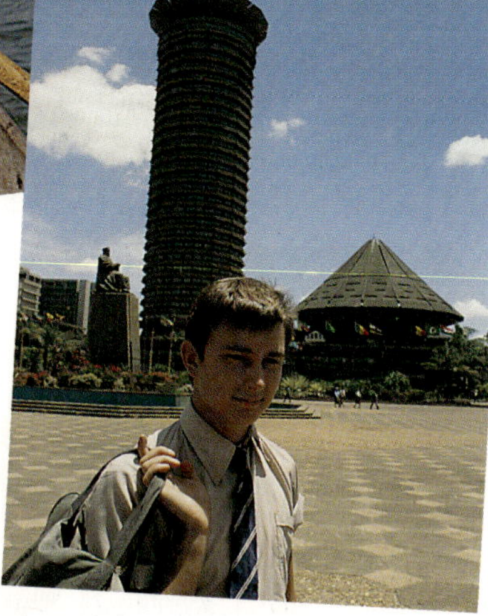

British

Activity 1

a) What do the photos in Source 1 suggest about the make-up of Kenya's population?

b) Use the words below to write a few sentences to describe the graph of population growth (Source 2):

steady growth | rapid rise | population doubled

Source 2
Population growth 1900 – 1993

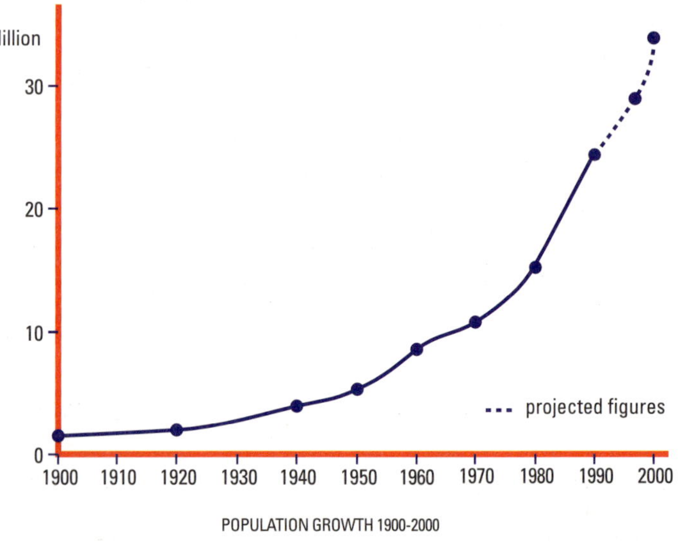

There are three main reasons why the population of Kenya is rising fast. **Infant mortality** is lower today than in the past. This means fewer children die from diseases. **Death rates** are also falling, so fewer people die. But the **birth rate** is still high.

Children are important to Kenyan people. Families are large. There are a number of reasons for this:

- Families expect their children to look after them in old age.
- Children help their parents on the land.
- Men move to the city to find jobs, so children are needed to help at home.
- Girls marry young, so they have more children.
- Today there is better health care, so there is less infant mortality.
- Better diet and a good water supply means people live longer.

Where do Kenya's people live?

Source 3

Population distribution and density

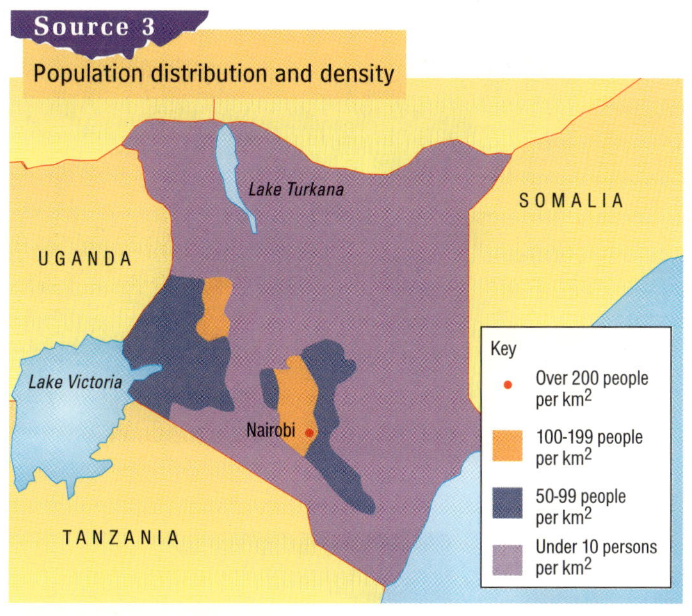

Source 4

Rainfall reliability

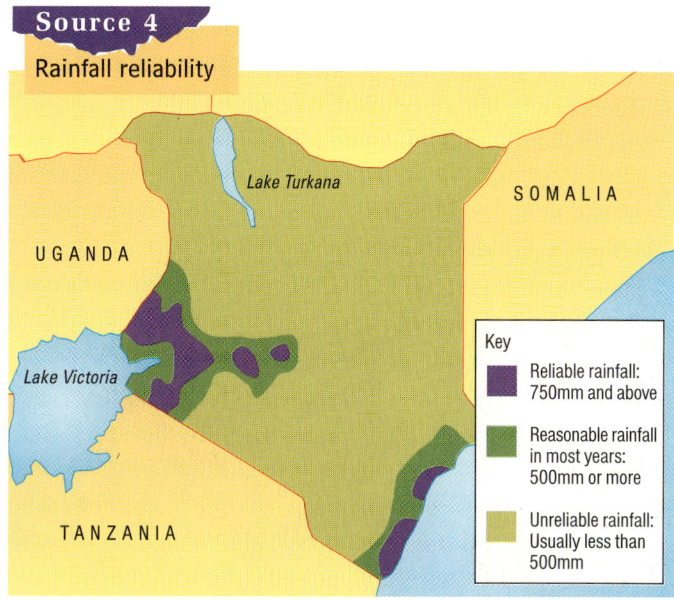

Activity 2

Look at Sources 3 and 4 and answer these questions:

a) Which is the most crowded area of Kenya?

b) Where do the fewest people live?

c) Which is Kenya's driest region?

d) Do you think there is a link between rainfall and population density?

Activity 3

These sentences describe what can happen when too many people move to an area. Use them to fill in the boxes on a copy of this flow chart. The last box has been done for you.

Trees are cut down for fuel. **People move to poor land.** **Not enough land for farming.** **Too many people.**

[ ] → [ ] → [ ] → [ ] → [This causes soil erosion]

Is it easy to solve the population problem?

The farmers say:

- The clinics are too far away, so we can't reach them easily.
- It's our tradition to have large families.
- We need more land and money.

What the government thinks:

- The population is growing too fast, so women must have fewer children.
- Family planning clinics will be made available.

Activity 4

a) What does the government minister want to do?

b) Do you agree with the minister? Explain why.

c) What do you think can be done to solve the farmer's problems?

Feeding people

How many people do you know who work on the land? In Kenya over 80 per cent of the population work on farms. Most farms are small, but there are also large estates.

Source 1

Farmland in Kiambu district

Source 2

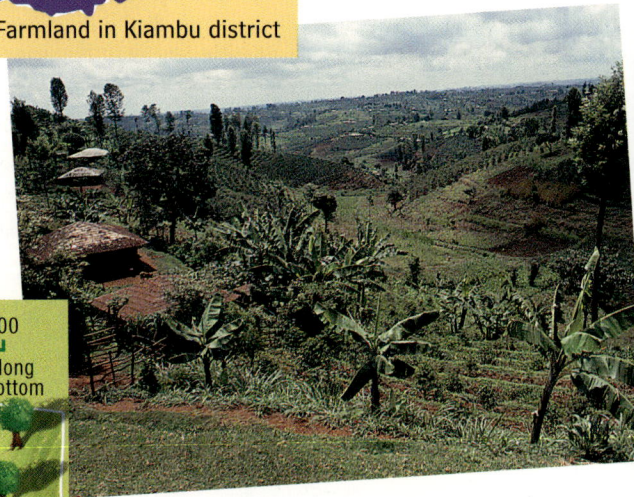

Land use on Mwaniki's farm

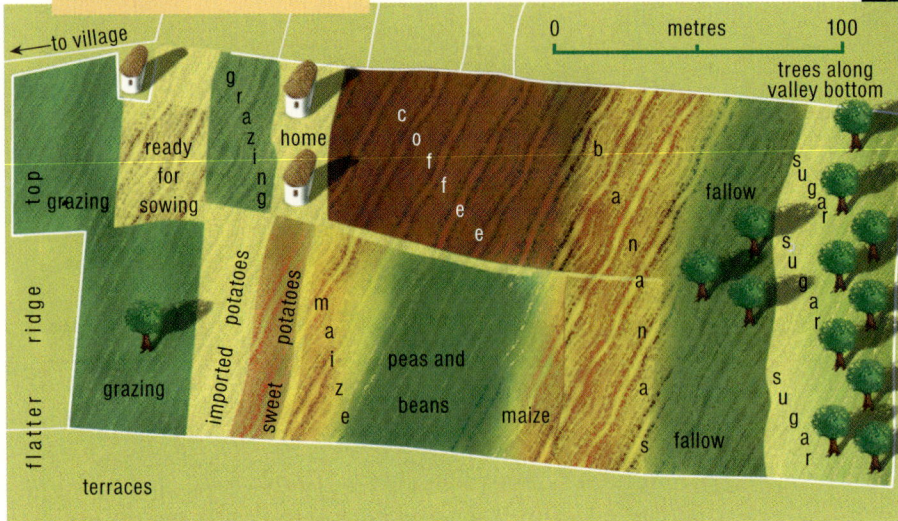

The Kikuyu people live on the uplands and slopes north of Nairobi. The land is high (over 2000 metres above sea-level). The rainfall is heavy and reliable, and the temperatures are cool. Here the soil is deep red and fertile, so farmers can grow a variety of crops (see Source 2). Many farmers earn a living by growing crops which they sell. These are called **cash crops**. They also grow food for their families and often keep several cows as well as chickens and goats.

Activity 1

Look at both the map and the photo (Sources 1 and 2).

a) Make a list of all the crops grown.

b) Which crops do you think are grown for the farmer's family?

c) Which crops are sold in the market?

Source 3

The farming year

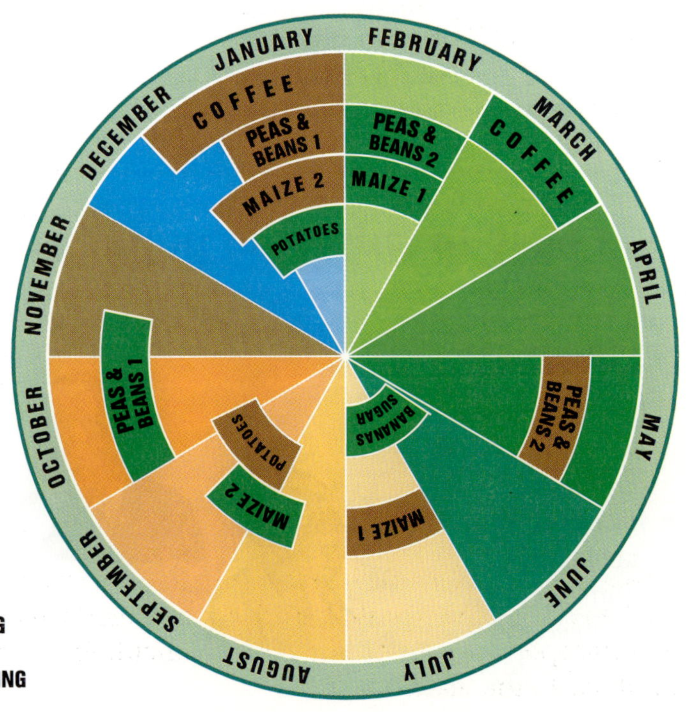

PLANTING

HARVESTING

Activity 2

Look at Source 3.

a) Which crops have to be sown each year?

b) How many crops of maize can be grown each year?

c) When is the busiest time for the farmer?

Do all people farm the land?

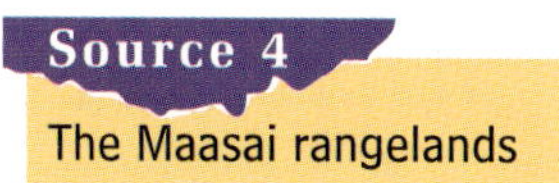
Source 4
The Maasai rangelands

Eighty per cent of Kenya is too dry for crop farming. South of Nairobi lie the rangelands where the Maasai people live. The Maasai are **nomads**. They travel over long distances with their cattle to find water during the dry season, but this is changing. The Maasai are being encouraged to settle down. It is believed that their cattle destroy the soil and bring diseases.

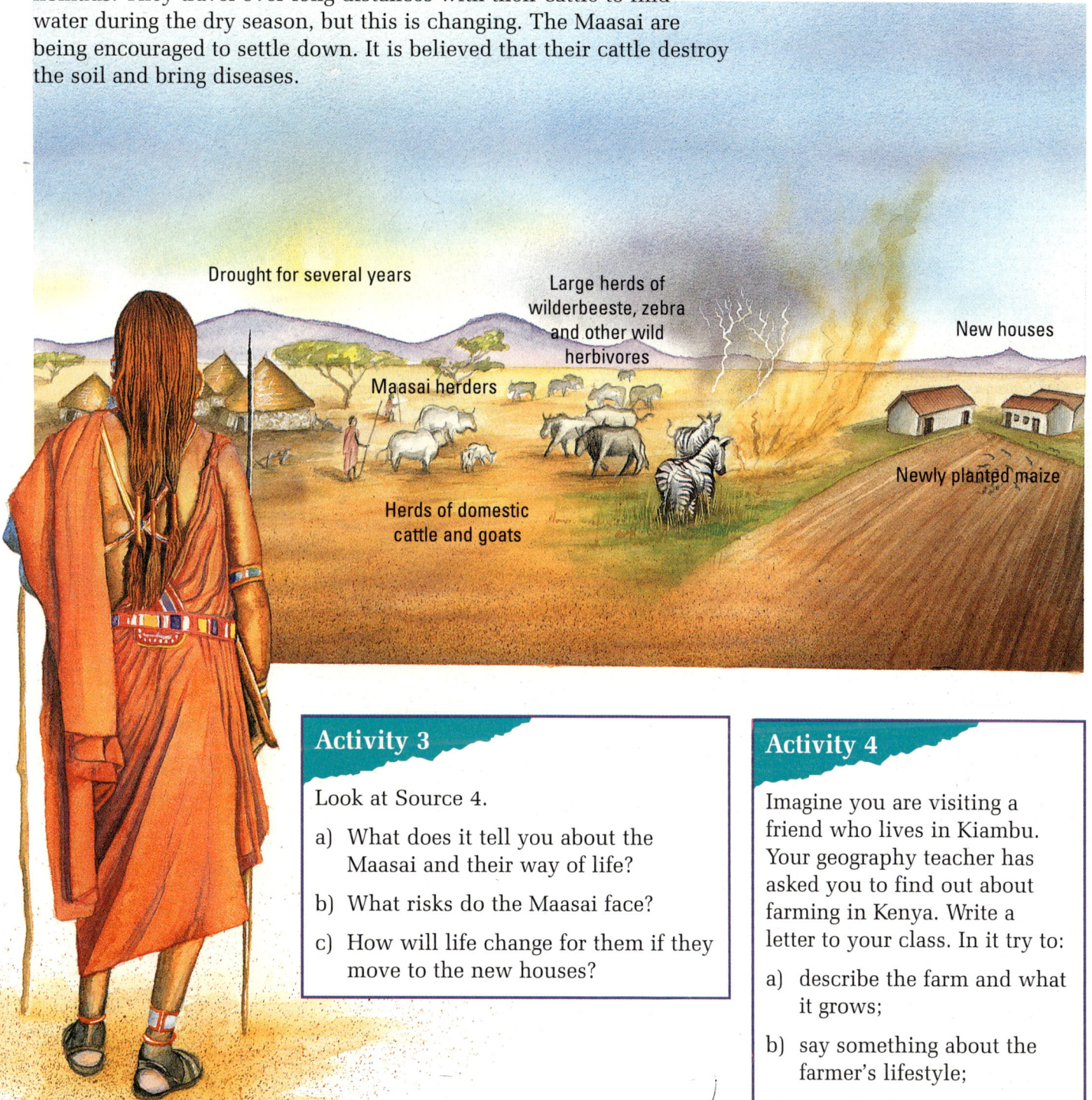

Activity 3

Look at Source 4.

a) What does it tell you about the Maasai and their way of life?

b) What risks do the Maasai face?

c) How will life change for them if they move to the new houses?

Activity 4

Imagine you are visiting a friend who lives in Kiambu. Your geography teacher has asked you to find out about farming in Kenya. Write a letter to your class. In it try to:

a) describe the farm and what it grows;

b) say something about the farmer's lifestyle;

c) note the farming problems for people in Kenya.

Use all the Sources on these pages to help you.

The biggest problem for Kenya's farmers is to grow enough food to feed an increasing population. There is a shortage of good, fertile land and transport is poor. This makes it difficult for farmers to get their products to the market.

Nairobi – city in the sun

Nairobi has grown to be a city of two million people in less than a hundred years. It began in 1899 as a camp and workshops for the railway which was being built from the coast to Lake Victoria. Today, Nairobi is Kenya's capital and the centre of its transport network. The city is home to many government buildings and several United Nations organisations as well as luxury hotels and offices. Nairobi is one of the largest cities in East Africa.

Activity 1

The photographs in Sources 2,3 and 4 show the different sides to life in Nairobi.

a) Which of the following words best describes each photograph?

modern	**rich**
luxurious	**attractive**
poor	**expensive**

b) Which area of the city would you like to visit? Say why.

Source 2
Some of Nairobi's luxury housing

The shanty areas

The map and Source 3 show that Nairobi has areas of poor housing. People move from the countryside to find work in Nairobi. When they arrive, these **migrants** have nowhere to live, so they have to build their own homes from whatever they can find. This might include pieces of wood and corrugated iron. An area of poor, home-made housing is called a **shanty town**. Often these areas are built quickly, so there is little time or money to provide electricity, water or sewerage. In some parts of the city the shanties are being improved. **Self-help groups** use the many skills the migrants have to build modern homes.

Activity 2

a) Why do you think people want to live in a big city like Nairobi?

b) Why are people forced to build their own homes?

c) What is a shanty town?

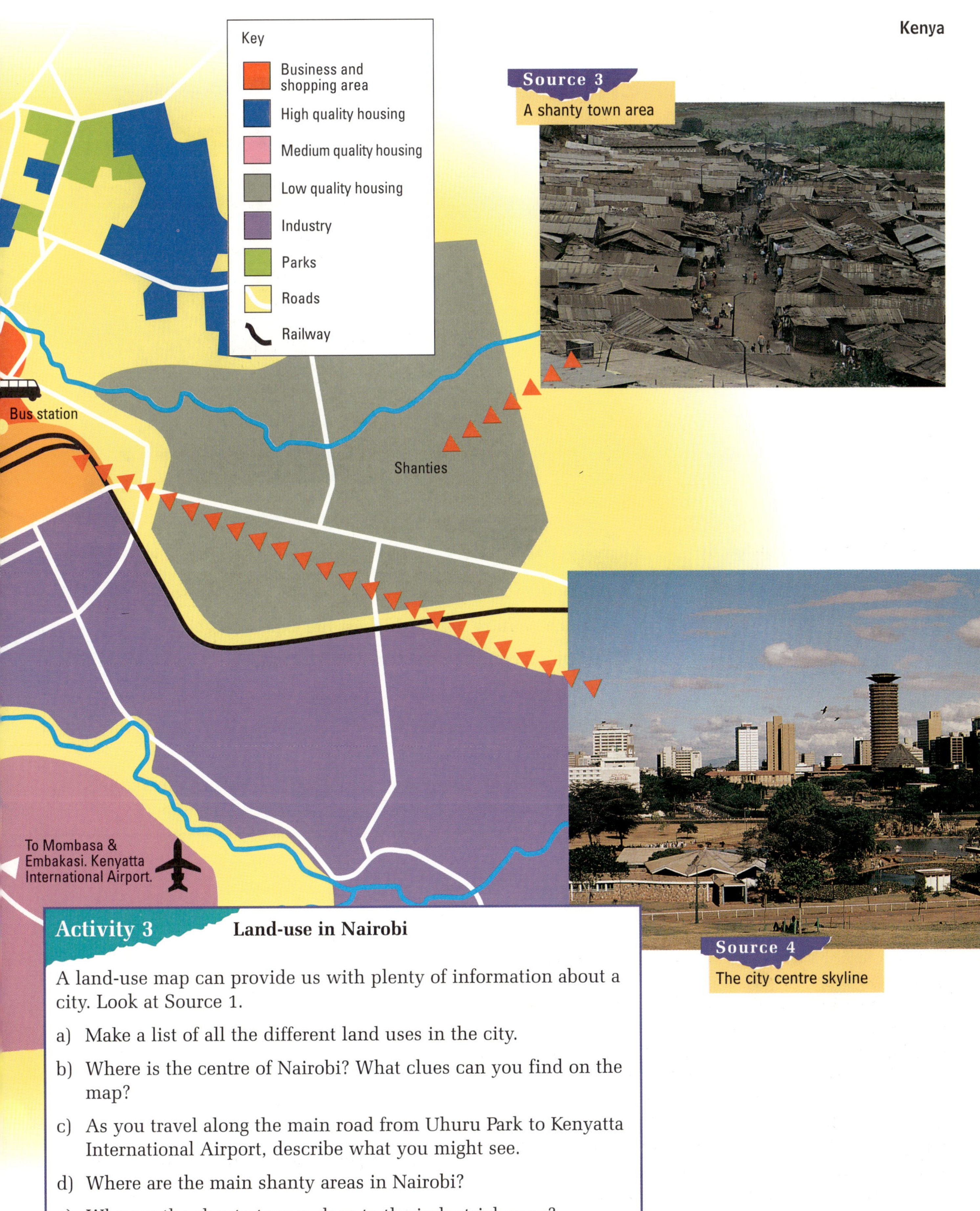

Source 3
A shanty town area

Source 4
The city centre skyline

Activity 3 Land-use in Nairobi

A land-use map can provide us with plenty of information about a city. Look at Source 1.

a) Make a list of all the different land uses in the city.

b) Where is the centre of Nairobi? What clues can you find on the map?

c) As you travel along the main road from Uhuru Park to Kenyatta International Airport, describe what you might see.

d) Where are the main shanty areas in Nairobi?

e) Why are the shanty towns close to the industrial areas?

The development ladder

Development can be measured in many different ways. Wealth (or money) is one measure, but quality of life is also important. If often seems easy to compare countries, but even wealthy countries have poor people - some people in the UK live in bad housing or are homeless, just as in Kenya.

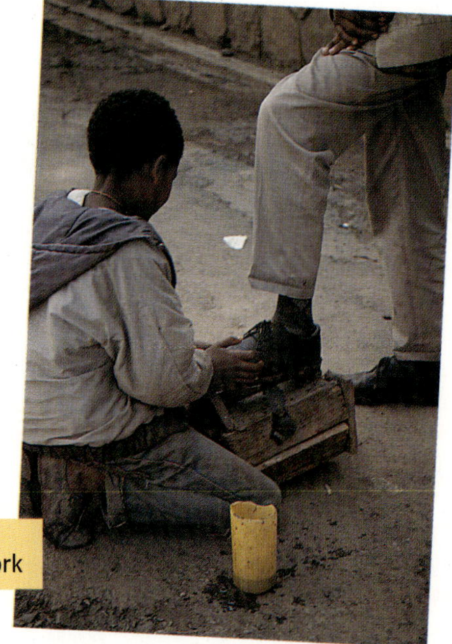

Source 1

A Kenyan child at work

Kenya is a **developing country**. People in Kenya are generally poorer than people in the UK, but there are other differences too. Look at Source 2 to discover some of these differences.

Activity 1

Study Source 2, then answer the following questions:

a) Which country has the highest life expectancy?

b) In which country does the average person earn less than $400?

c) Where are people likely to eat more food?

d) Infant mortality shows how many babies die. Where is this highest?

e) Can you think of any ways in which life in Kenya might be better than life in the UK?

Source 2

The UK and Kenya compared

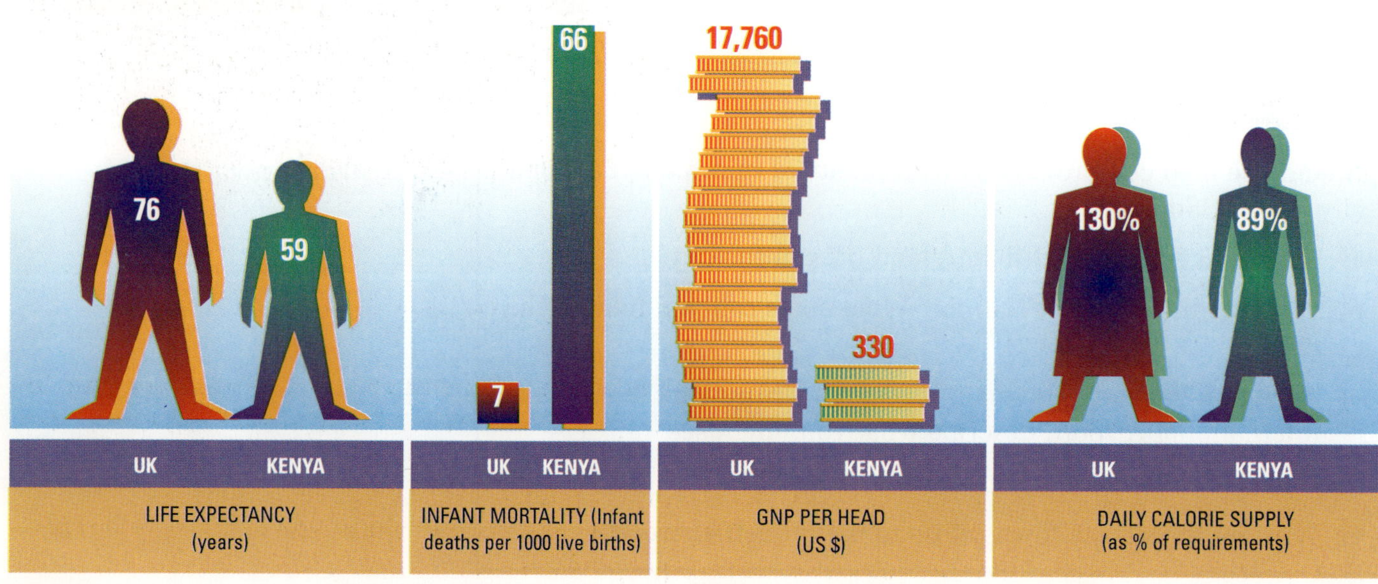

What is life like for Kenyans?

Source 3
Mary

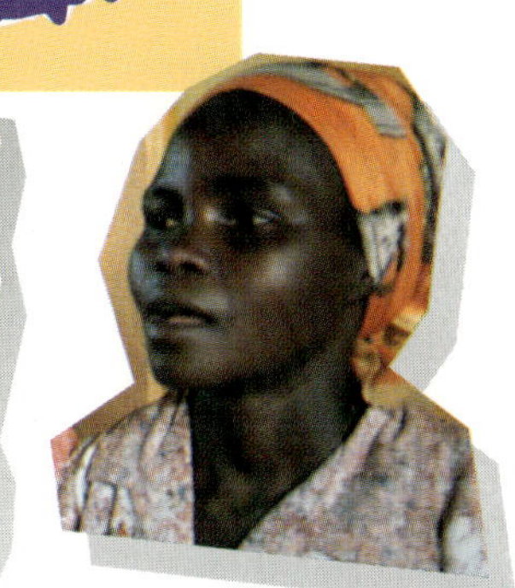

'I work for a charity in Nairobi. We help families in the shanty towns. I train people to set up their own businesses and raise money for equipment. I am married with four children. My husband, Ben, is a government planner. We all live in a brick bungalow with a garden three miles from the city centre. At weekends we drive to Kiambu to see my parents.'

Source 4
Henry

'I drive a *matatu*. The *matatu* belongs to my boss, but I hope to buy one soon. I live in a stone house with my second wife. There isn't enough space here for my first wife and family, so I go back to my village to visit them. We don't have water in the house and my wife uses charcoal for cooking outside. I sometimes do odd jobs for a local garage. I need the extra money for my oldest children.'

Source 5
A *matatu!*

OVERLOADING IS THE ONLY WAY TO MAKE...

Activity 2

a) Look at the photograph of Mary (Source 3). Does she seem rich or poor? From what she says, what do you think her life is like?

b) Look at the cartoon (Source 5). What is a *matatu*?

c) How and why does Henry (Source 4) make extra money?

d) What are the main differences in Henry's and Mary's lifestyles?

Development today

Even though there have been big improvements in Kenya's economy, most Kenyans are relatively poor. Small areas of the country are well developed, but much of the country still needs better roads and reliable, clean water supplies. For the majority of people life in Kenya is difficult.

'Jambo Tembo'

Conservation, tourism and national parks

Kenya's economy depends heavily on tourism. It has two great attractions which attract visitors who bring much-needed money into the country: its scenery and its wildlife.

Source 2

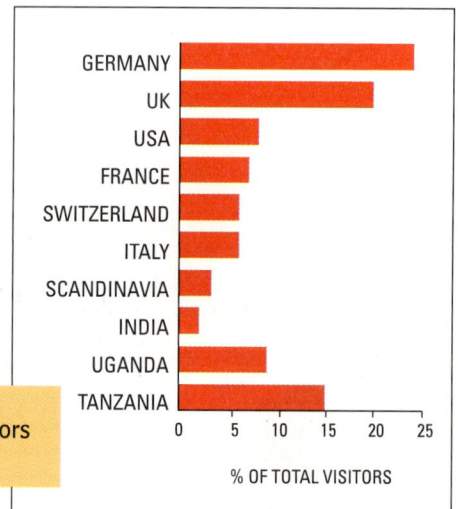

Where do Kenya's visitors come from?

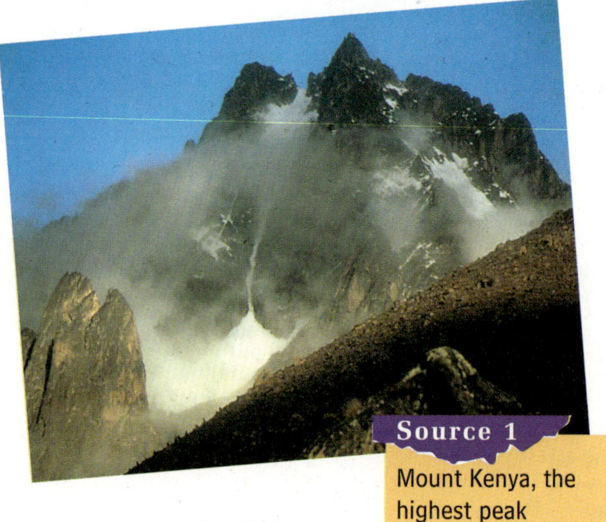

Source 1

Mount Kenya, the highest peak

Activity 1 **Where do the tourists come from?**

Look at Sources 2, 3 and 4 then answer these questions:

a) Where do most of Kenya's tourists come from?

b) Why do you think so many Europeans visit Kenya?

c) From which African countries do people visit Kenya? Use an atlas to find out why.

Why visit Kenya?

'We have come to see the animals.'

'I want sunshine and swimming.'

'Nowhere else has such a variety of scenery with such a good climate.'

'My grandparents lived here and told me wonderful tales.'

Safaris are the most popular type of holiday in Kenya. They are fairly cheap. Most tourists spend time in one of the national parks like Amboseli or the Maasai Mara, then visit the coast. Almost one million people visited Kenya in 1992.

More tourists are now visiting remote districts like Lake Turkana. Mount Kenya (see Source 1) is also popular with climbers and walkers.

Source 3

Beaches and hotels

The downside ...

There has been a fall in the number of visitors to Kenya since 1992. The headlines help explain why.

Gunmen kill tourists in the Maasai Mara

VISITORS ROBBED IN NAIROBI ATTACK

Tourist buses are frightening animals

TREES CHOPPED DOWN TO MAKE WAY FOR HOTELS

What is being done?

Tourists have been so frightened that security has been tightened in the national parks to protect them. The Kenyan government is also encouraging tourists to visit the less crowded areas.

Source 4

The 'big five'. Kenyan wildlife popular with tourists.

Poaching is a big problem. It has reduced the number of elephants, and there are almost no rhinoceros left in Kenya (Source 4). Some Kenyans think of animals as food or as money. Ivory tusks are taken from the elephants and are sold to traders in Japan and Hong Kong.

A world ban on the sale of elephant products means that poaching for ivory tusks has almost stopped in Kenya. Today the herds are beginning to increase again.

Activity 2

You will need: an atlas, some holiday brochures for Kenya, a piece of A3 paper, and colouring pencils.

Design a poster about tourism in Kenya. You should include:

- the main places to visit and things to do;
- some information on each place;
- some good *and* bad points of tourism.

Trade and aid

No country can produce all its own goods and services. This means that countries need to trade with one another. Trade involves **imports** and **exports**.

- *Imports* are the goods and services **bought** from another country.
- *Exports* are the goods and services **sold** to another country.

Problems can occur when a country buys more goods than it sells. This is called a **trade deficit**.

Source 1

Kenya's major trading partners, 1992

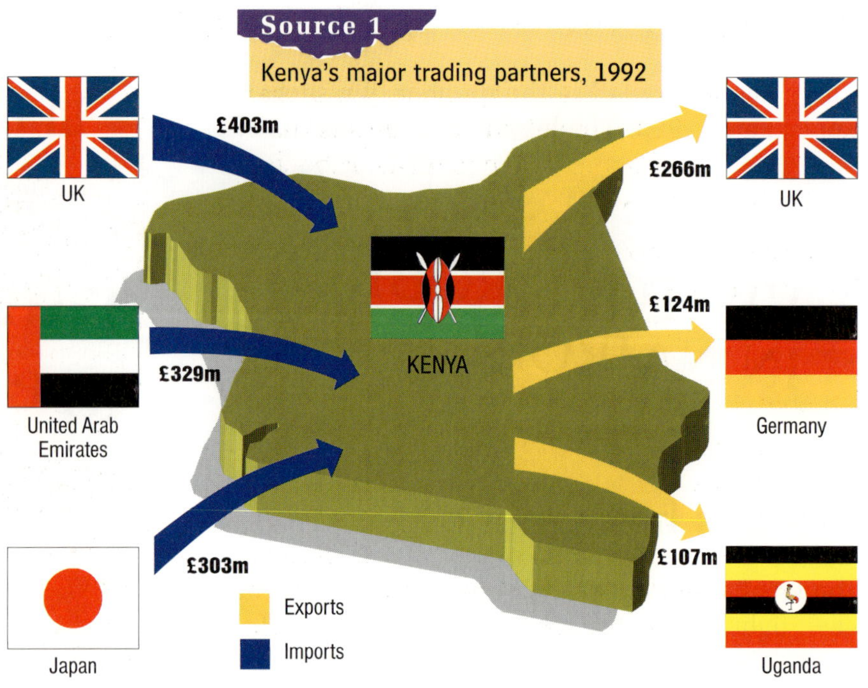

Exports and imports

Trade has played an important part in Kenya's development. For many years its exports consisted mostly of coffee, tea and sisal (used for making rope and sacking). Today, though it exports a greater range of products. Imported goods include manufactured items and crude oil. Look at Sources 2 and 3.

Activity 1

Look at Source 1 and answer the following questions:

a) Which three countries sell goods to Kenya?

b) Which country sells the most goods to Kenya?

c) To which countries does Kenya export its goods?

d) Add up the value of Kenya's imports, then add up the value of its exports. Does Kenya buy or sell more goods?

Source 2

Exports

Source 3

Imports

Buying too much … selling too little

Kenya's problem is that it buys more goods than it can sell. It has a **trade deficit**. This means that there is little money to improve roads, schools or the health services.

One way of improving Kenya's trade balance is by increasing its exports. Today Kenyan farmers are being encouraged to grow vegetables. Some are sold in UK supermarkets. Look at Source 4. How many of these vegetables do you eat?

Some of the money we pay in the shops for Kenyan vegetables helps farmers in Kenya to pay for seeds, fertiliser and new equipment. Most of it is spent on transporting and storing the produce. Everyone involved in getting the goods onto supermarket shelves must make some profits for their efforts.

Source 4

A variety of Kenyan products

Source 5

Health care is one way that aid money is spent

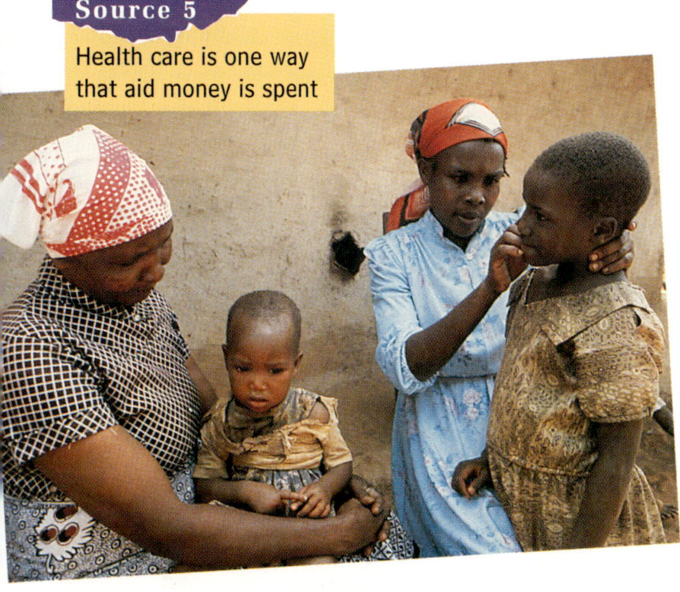

Aid

Another way that Kenya can solve its trade problem is through aid. Countries such as the UK, the United States of America and Japan, as well as the European Union, have provided aid. Much of this money is spent on projects to improve water supplies, schools and health care.

Organisations like CARE, OXFAM, CAFOD and Save the Children also work in Kenya to help local people (see Source 5).

Aid is important, but Kenya will need more small industries if it is to export more goods and improve its trade balance.

Group Activity

Work with a partner for this activity. You both work for the Department of Trade and Industry in London, and have been sent to Kenya to write a report on trade. You need to think about the following:

- Who does Kenya trade with?
- Which goods does it import and export?
- What problems does it have?
- How do you think its trade problems can be solved?

Now write your report. Use all the sources on pages 86 and 87 to help you.

Who should have the aid?

CAFOD

A decision-making exercise

Aid for developing countries may be given through governments, or agencies like the United Nations. Many small projects are funded by charities such as Save the Children and Oxfam. Help also comes from church-based agencies like CAFOD, the Catholic Fund for Overseas Development. All these are called non-governmental organisations or NGOs.

CAFOD's development programme aims to help people themselves. It supports projects among very poor people, and tries to tackle the causes of poverty, hunger, sickness and oppression. Projects include:

- providing clean water supplies;
- improving health care for all;
- increasing food production;
- supporting women in poor communities;
- helping more people to read and write.

Activity 1

Look carefully at the list above. Which do you think are CAFOD's most important projects? Rewrite the list with your most important projects first.

There are many different ways that a charity can help. Sources 1, 2 and 3 show three of them.

Source 1

Women's groups in Nairobi

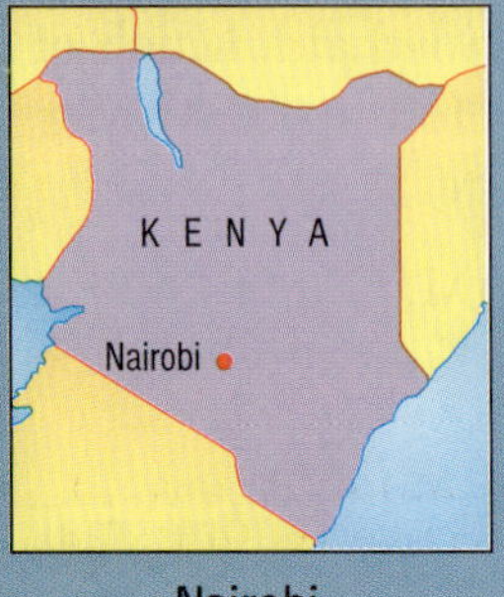

Nairobi

Scheme 1

Help for women's groups in Nairobi

Money is needed to pay for training in tailoring, pottery, basket work and simple business skills. This would help many women who live with large families in very poor conditions to support themselves and their families.

Cost: £10 000

Women basket makers

Source 2

Water in Kitui

Kitui

Scheme 2

Kitui water programme

Local workers need training in conservation methods. Wells, roof tanks and simple storage systems are needed. The district is suffering from drought and soil erosion. It is densely populated. Most people work on the land. There is little other employment.

Cost: £10 000

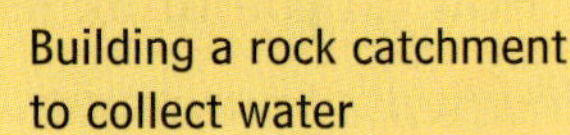

Building a rock catchment to collect water

Source 3

Health in Laisamis

Laisamis

Scheme 3

Health care programme for Laisamis district

Two nurses and a translator are needed for the mobile clinics which help the nomadic Rendille and Samburu people on the edge of the desert in northern Kenya. The clinics provide vaccinations, health care training and baby care. Most of the people live up to 90 km from the nearest hospital.

Cost: £10 000

A mobile health team

Group Activity

Imagine that you work in London for CAFOD. You have £20,000 to give to projects in Kenya in the next year. The money must be allocated according to CAFOD's aims. Look at Sources 1, 2 and 3.

a) What aspects of community life does each scheme help to develop? To help you to decide, draw up a table like the one below.

Scheme	(A) Water	(B) Health	(C) Food	(D) Women	(E) Adult Education	Total	Weighting	New Total
Women's Groups, Nairobi	–	X	X	X	X	4		
Kitui water programme								
Health care, Laisamis								

Scheme 1 does not provide water, but may improve health, increase food supplies and it does help women. The women have to be able to read and write so it will help with adult literacy. We can put crosses (X) in four columns (B, C, D and E). The total (4) is entered in the correct column.

b) Now try to assess the other schemes in the same way. When you have done both of them, work out the total for each scheme. You could now decide which projects you should spend money on.

c) Do you think all the projects are equally important? Discuss the projects with your friends. Some people might think that improving water supplies is more important than feeding people. If you think this, double the number of crosses in the water column (A) to show that this is an important scheme. Then add up the scores again. This is called **weighting** the score. Work through the table again, weighting the scores according to how important you think each scheme is.

d) Now you have placed the projects in your order of importance. Try to divide up the money (£20,000) according to this order. Which projects would you support, and why?

e) What would you say to the schemes you decide not to support?

Development

Which of the following countries do you think is the richest: Brazil, Kenya, Italy, Japan or the UK? Which is the poorest country? Try writing them out in order, starting with the richest country first.

One way of exploring differences between countries is to look at data or information. Source 1 gives some facts and figures about these five countries.

	Brazil	Italy	Japan	Kenya	UK
Area in km^2	846505	294068	376508	569696	241595
Population in millions	155.3	57.2	125	27	58.4
Population density in millions	18.3	194	33	47.3	241
Natural increase	1.7	0	0.3	3.3	0.2
Life expectancy	67	77	79	59	76
GNP per capita	$2770	$20,510	$28,220	$330	$17,760
No of TV's per 100 of population	21.5	42	62	1.0	43

Source 1
Development indicators

This information can be used to tell us how rich or poor a country is. One important measure of wealth is **Gross National Product** or GNP. This is the average amount of money made by a country from selling its products. Other differences to look out for include:

- **natural increase:** shows how fast the population is growing;
- **population per km^2:** indicates how crowded or empty a country is;
- **life expectancy:** a measure of how long people are expected to live.

Activity 1

a) Study Source 1. Look at the data for GNP and check if your list of rich and poor countries is correct.

b) Do you live in a rich or a poor country? (The map in Source 4 may help you.)

c) What other facts and figures could be used to compare countries?

d) Do you think wealth is the best way to compare countries?

Source 2
Britain

The information in Source 1 shows us some important indicators of wealth, but we can also compare the quality of life from place to place. The **quality of life** includes things which are personal to us. For example, is our environment clean and safe? Do we feel happy living there?

Source 3
Mombasa, Kenya

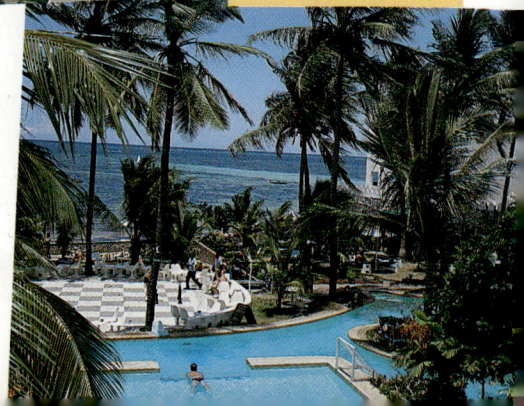

Activity 2

Look at Sources 2 and 3.

a) What words would you use to describe each photograph?

b) What is the quality of life like in each environment?

Source 4

Rich and poor countries of the world

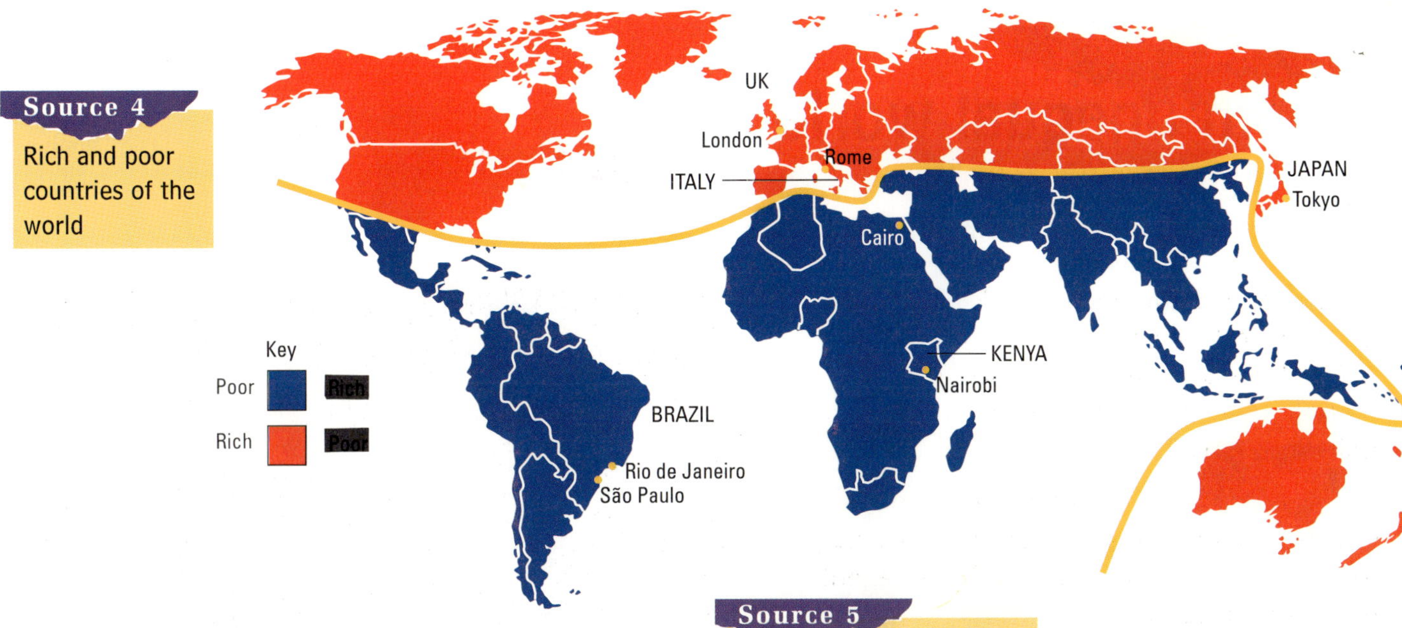

Source 5

The developed world …

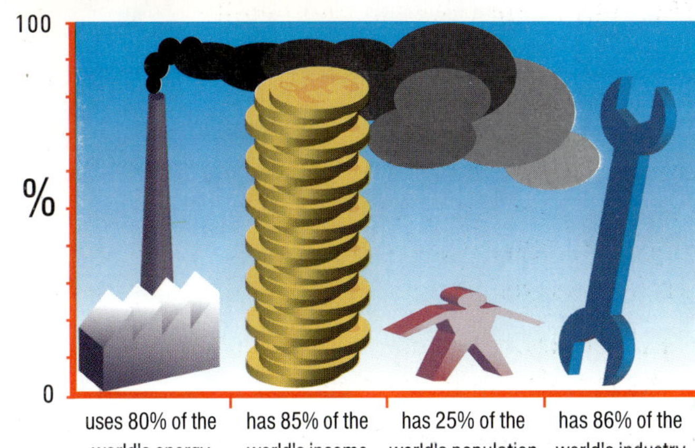

Activity 3

a) Look at Source 4. Are the following sentences true or false?

- Japan belongs to the developing world.
- Kenya is in one of the richest continents on earth.
- Most people live in the developed world.
- 86 per cent of the world's industry is in the developed world.

b) What do you notice about where the rich (developed) and poor (developing) countries are? Write two simple sentences. Begin like this:

'Developing countries are mainly found in …'

'Developed countries are mainly found in …'

Activity 4

It is often said that developement takes place unevenly. What evidence can you find for this in Sources 1, 4 and 5?

A world of information, but can we use it?

Activity 5

Many people do not know how to measure the differences between rich and poor countries. Oxfam wants you to produce a poster titled 'Measuring development'. Use the information in Sources 1 and 4 to help you.

a) Before you start, think about how we decide which are the developed/developing nations. Explain this in the first section.

b) Now, choose two different countries – one rich, one poor. Write about each country. Use some facts and figures to show how developed it is. You could include a simple map.

An unequal world

Study these two photographs carefully. Which do you think is of a developing country and which is of a developed country?

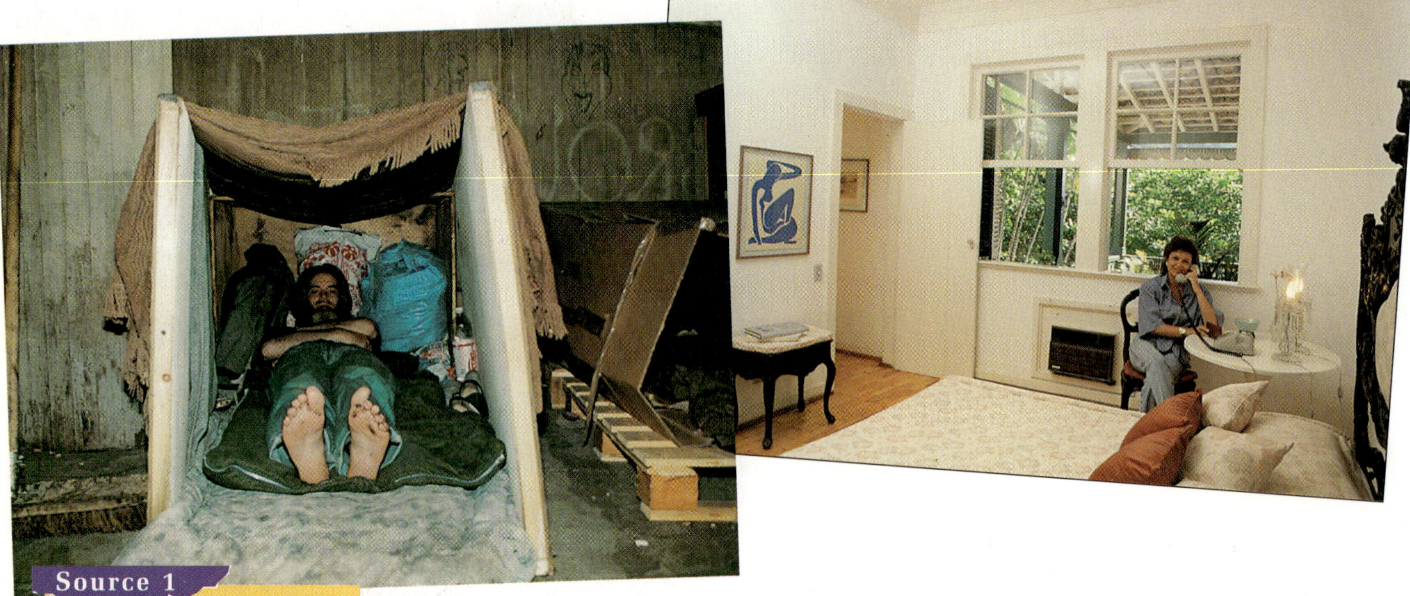

Source 1
Developed or developing?

Source 2
Developed or developing?

It's not what you might expect. The photograph of the homeless person is from the streets of London. The second photograph is of a Brazilian housewife who lives in a modern furnished apartment in Brasília, the capital of Brazil.

At times it is easy to forget that there are often huge differences between rich and poor people **within** countries as well as **between** countries. The popular image of Brazil is one of poverty, but there are wealthy people too. Take Anna for example (Source 2).

Source 3
Anna

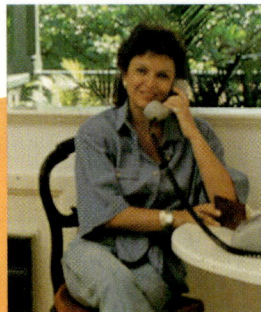

My name is Anna. I'm 35 and I live in Brasília, the capital of Brazil. I am married to a wealthy banker and we have two children. They go to a private school in Brasília. We live in a large apartment close to the city centre. It has four bedrooms, two bathrooms and all the modern conveniences, including a high security entry-phone system. A maid helps around the house and we take frequent holidays abroad.

Activity 1

Look at Sources 2 and 3.

a) What do they tell you about Anna and her lifestyle?

b) What evidence is there in the photo that Anna and her family are wealthy?

Inequality in the UK

If you walk through any of Britain's large cities, you may well find homeless people sleeping in shop doorways or on the streets. There are many reasons why people in developed countries can become poor.

Activity 2

Read about Ian in Source 4, then answer these questions:

a) Why did Ian become homeless?

b) How does he survive on the streets of London?

c) Do you think he wants to be homeless?

Activity 3

Imagine you are either Anna or Ian.

a) Write a few sentences describing your typical day

b) What do you think are the biggest differences in the lifestyles of Anna and Ian? Discuss this in small groups.

What can be done?

Six people were asked what they would do to help homeless people. Here is what they said:

- Give money to a charity like 'Shelter' which helps homeless people.
- Make the Government spend more money on hostels.
- Do nothing – it's not my problem.
- Open more soup kitchens to provide food for the homeless.
- Young people like Ian should stay at home. It's up to his family to help him.
- Make rented housing much cheaper.

Source 4

Ian

I'm Ian, and I live on the streets. I left my home in Glasgow to come to London, but when I arrived I had no job, no money and no contacts. I had no choice but to sleep rough. I got a sleeping bag from a church but have to beg to get money for food. The truth is it's easy to become homeless, even if you think you are well prepared.

Activity 4

a) Reread the last section 'What can be done?' Six ways of helping homeless people are suggested. Which do you think is the most important? Rewrite the list in order of importance.

b) Say why the two solutions at the top of your list are most important.

Links in a chain

Think about the many different gadgets you may have in your home: TVs, video-recorders, radios, personal stereos. Have you ever thought about where these products are made? Consider the personal stereo pictured below. Take a close look at it. Where is it made? In which countries do you think personal stereos are used? Now take a look at Source 2.

Source 1

Where is this made?

Source 2

Personal stereos are popular all over the world, including Kenya!

Many items we use, like personal stereos, or products we eat, like chocolate, are international. As well as being known all over the world, they use ingredients or raw materials from more than one country. **Raw materials** or component parts often have to be **assembled** to make the things we buy. This means that many places are connected like links in a chain.

Think about how many countries might be involved in producing a bar of chocolate: cocoa is grown in Ghana, and sugar cane comes from the islands in the West Indies. These ingredients are combined with others at a factory in the UK, and then the finished bars of chocolate are shipped all over the world to be sold, eaten and enjoyed. Again, several places in different continents are linked in a kind of chain (Source 3).

Source 3

The international chocolate chain

Activity 1

Seven raw materials are listed below. For each one, there is a clue which should help you identify the country which the raw material comes from. Each country is marked on Source 4.

Cotton: comes from a country which has its coastline on the Indian Ocean.

Rubber: the capital city of this country is Lagos.

Cocoa: a West African country to the West of Nigeria.

Oil: capital city and country share the same name in Central America.

Beef: a large country south of Brazil.

Wool: the home of Neighbours and Kangaroos.

Gold: a country on the southern tip of Africa.

Choose your countries from this list:

Argentina, Australia, Ghana, India, Mexico, Nigeria, South Africa

a) Name one product made using each of these raw materials.

b) Which of these raw materials (if any) could you live without?

Source 4
World map

Group Activity

Work in small groups to produce a poster. You will need:

- a blank map of the world.
- A3 paper;

Choose a product such as a chocolate bar, breakfast cereal, or computer game. Identify its ingredients, components or raw materials from the wrapper or packing materials, and work out which countries they come from. Find out where the product is made and is sold. Mark all these countries on your map.

Now, design a poster for the product you chose to explain the 'links in the chain' which you have discovered.

Index